Born, Not Made

Born, Not Made

The Entrepreneurial Personality

James L. Fisher and James V. Koch

PRAEGER

Westport, Connecticut
London

Library of Congress Cataloging-in-Publication Data

Fisher, James L. (James Lee), 1931–
    Born, not made : the entrepreneurial personality / James L. Fisher and James V. Koch.
        p.   cm.
    Includes bibliographical references and index.
    ISBN: 978–0–313–35050–4 (alk. paper)
    1. Entrepreneurship.   2. Entrepreneurship—Research.   3. Business enterprises.
I. Koch, James V., 1942–   II. Title.
    HB615.F57   2008
    338′.04—dc22   2008020076

British Library Cataloguing in Publication Data is available.

Library of Congress Catalog Card Number: 2008020076
ISBN: 978–0–313–35050–4

First published in 2008

Praeger Publishers, 88 Post Road West, Westport, CT 06881
An imprint of Greenwood Publishing Group, Inc.
www.praeger.com

Printed in the United States of America

The paper used in this book complies with the
Permanent Paper Standard issued by the National
Information Standards Organization (Z39.48–1984).

10 9 8 7 6 5 4 3 2 1

Contents

Chapter 1

The Entrepreneurial Personality

Being on the tightrope is living; everything else is waiting.
—Attributed to Karl Wallenda, high-wire artist.

I could have lost everything and I almost did several times.
—A West Coast CEO, 2004.

[R]isk takers almost always recognize one another as brothers and sisters genetically linked by their desire to experience the uncertainties of the edge.
—Stephen Lyng, *Edgework: The Sociology of Risk-Taking*, 2005.

Entrepreneurs are different, and this book is about the nature of those differences. Individuals who found their own firms view the world and its challenges differently than most others. They're more optimistic, extroverted, energetic, self-confident, and visionary than the typical person and, critically, willing to take more risks. They'll often risk their personal financial fortunes and sometimes even their own lives in order to pursue their dreams. Entrepreneurship and risk-taking seem to be in their blood.

Even though most entrepreneurs (perhaps 75 percent) eventually fail, they are seldom deterred. Like determined boxers who have taken an uppercut and been knocked to the canvas, many of them get back on their feet and come back for more. Serial entrepreneurs, whether successful or not, often found new firms over and over again, or repeatedly develop new ventures and technologies. Inventor Thomas Edison was responsible for more than 1,000 patents in his lifetime and continued to generate remarkable innovations until his death, even though hundreds of his ideas led him to discouraging dead ends. Walt Disney, an unsuccessful student as a youth, bounced through a series of ill-fated ventures before beating the odds with movies such as *Snow White* and developments such as Disneyland. Disney ignored the advice both of bankers and colleagues as he plunged ahead with these initiatives.

If individuals such as Edison and Disney are distinctive, then what really is singular about them and other entrepreneurs? What motivated Fred Smith, the founder of Federal Express, to transform the idea he originally developed for a college term paper into a *Fortune 500* firm known around the world? Smith did so despite the oft-repeated, perhaps apocryphal wisdom that his professor assigned a C grade to the term paper because the professor regarded the idea as unrealistic.

USUALLY BORN, NOT MADE

Both genetic evidence and survey data support the notion that a substantial proportion of entrepreneurial behavior is genetically determined. Put simply, much entrepreneurial behavior is inherited. The *entrepreneurial personality* that drives risk-taking, innovation, and the founding of new firms isn't something one can buy from the shelf at Wal-Mart or Macy's. Nor can the salient features of an entrepreneurial personality easily be taught or learned, whether at Harvard or even from one's parents.

The truth is that far more entrepreneurs, the people who found their own firms and put themselves, their resources, and even their families at risk, are born rather than made. The confident driven individuals who become entrepreneurs typically have different genetic endowments than those who are not entrepreneurial. And these distinctive genetic endowments tend to produce the distinctive personality traits that characterize entrepreneurs.

Italian immigrant Amadeo Giannini, who founded the organization that ultimately evolved into the Bank of America, may not have been a "hypomanic" (a description of entrepreneurs favored by Gartner, 2005), and certainly was not highly educated, but he was a driven, highly competitive individual who was doing vegetable produce deals in California markets before he even became a teenager. Shortly thereafter, he developed the magnificent vision that matured into the Bank of America.

Resort timeshare developer David Siegel began to deliver newspapers at age four. A few years later, his father, who owned a grocery store, gave him a box of bubble gum, which Siegel proceeded to cut into ten pieces to resell (Kroll, 2007). Steve Case, the founder of AOL, was only six years old when he began to sell lime juice from trees in his backyard. When only twelve years old, Michael Dell started a small company that sold stamps to collectors. A few years later he launched Dell Computers from his college dorm room. Walt Disney earned his "at risk" spurs as a poker player while a teenage soldier at the close of World War I.

Yes, entrepreneurs are different. Most are hardwired genetically to react differently than other individuals to external stimuli that portray risk, danger, excitement, and change. Depending upon the personality trait, up to 60 percent of a trait may be inherited from one's ancestors. Individuals who inherit certain gene sequences are simply more likely to become entrepreneurs than others. As Canli (2006) put it, there exists a "biological basis for temperament." McCrae (2004) goes further and argues that the source of personality traits is entirely biological.

Indeed, entrepreneurial activity is a matter of probabilities and tendencies.[1] Some individuals simply are more likely to undertake entrepreneurial activities by virtue of their personality traits. In turn, entrepreneurial personality traits (optimism, extroversion, high energy levels, self-confidence, competitiveness, a motivating vision, and willingness to take and even seek out risks) have a significant genetic basis.

It is axiomatic that one can buy an education, but one cannot buy genes. Like height, one cannot purchase entrepreneurial genes that somehow are injected into one's body, miraculously transforming personality and character.

Height as a human characteristic provides a useful analogy. The average National Basketball Association (NBA) basketball player is about seven inches taller than the typical adult male American. You can't teach height; either you're tall or you're not. But, players can be taught to make the most of their height (or lack thereof) and hopefully learn to avoid unproductive competitive situations (it's usually not smart for a $5'11''$ guard to attempt to dunk on Houston Rocket center Yao Ming, who is $7'6''$). Practice may not make perfect, but it often helps overcome some genetic deficiencies. In addition, inspired coaching may mold or alter some players' attitudes so that they pass the ball more readily, play team defense, avoid destructive criticism of their teammates, and the like.

Even so, at the end of the day, genetic gifts have a powerful influence upon who can play well in the NBA. If that were not so, then the two authors of this book, who over the years have fancied themselves as "pretty good" amateur basketball players, would have had long and successful NBA careers. Intellectually, both of us understand what it takes to be a successful NBA player and we're willing to practice. Alas! We simply don't have the ability to take advantage of our knowledge.

In the NBA, then, genetic endowments exert a great influence over game play, and players with the gifts of a Michael Jordan are rare. So also it is in the realm of entrepreneurship. Some individuals are not well situated to become entrepreneurs, but not simply because they lack financing, or have insufficient education and knowledge, or are badly located geographically. It is their own personality traits, which are at least partially dependent upon their own genetic endowments that reduce the chance they will ever become entrepreneurs.

Many studies indicate that entrepreneurs tend to be enthusiastic, extroverted individuals (MacCrimmon and Wehring, 1986; Miner, 1997a, b; Pervin, Cervone, and John, 2004). Extroversion is a personality trait that has been demonstrated to have a significant heritable, genetic basis (Plomin, DeFries, McClearn, and McGuffin, 2001; Plomin, DeFries, Craig and McGuffin, 2003; Ridley, 2003; Canli, 2006). Either a person is extroverted or he is not. If a specific individual is not extroverted, then this does not mean he cannot become a successful entrepreneur. It does mean he is less likely to do so.

Are all entrepreneurs extroverted? No, our own survey data and interviews covering 234 CEOs (Chief Executive Officers, 102 of whom were entrepreneurs and founded their own firm) demonstrate that some entrepreneurs, even some very successful ones, have been somewhat introverted. Rather, introversion (and for that matter, other personality traits such as risk aversion and a lack of receptivity to change) reduces the probability that an individual will act entrepreneurially, whether as the founder of a business, as a politician, as a policeman, or even as a college president.

The issue devolves into an analysis of probabilities and tendencies. Genetic endowments do not rigidly determine entrepreneurial behavior; however, it is clear they do influence it significantly. There are genetic bases for human behavior, but genes only "constrain" certain outcomes (Kagan's 2000 terminology). Personality traits influence, but typically do not prohibit, a wide range of behaviors, including choice of occupation and one's willingness to assume risks. Hence, it seems safe to say that most U.S. Marine lance corporals who volunteer for service in Afghanistan or Iraq have different personality traits than most Roman Catholic nuns teaching elementary school in Dubuque, Iowa. This doesn't mean, however, that there may not be a few exceptions to this generalization. It's a matter of probabilities.

Our interest (and that of our readers) is in focusing on those aspects of personality that appear to be crucial to entrepreneurial activity and later success. If certain genetically influenced personality traits are associated with entrepreneurship, then many individuals and organizations will be better off if they are aware of those relationships.

WHAT IS AN ENTREPRENEUR?

Casson, the foremost historian of entrepreneurship, remarks that "The term entrepreneur, which most people recognize as meaning someone who organizes and assumes the risk of a business in return for the profits" (1993, p. 631), appears to have been first used by the eighteenth century Irish economist Richard Cantillon. Cantillon's French descent perhaps led him to construct this new English word based upon the French verb, *entreprendre*, meaning, "to undertake." Hence, an entrepreneur is one who starts an enterprise and assumes risk.

WHAT'S AT STAKE?

Many things in our world function on the basis of small differences in probability. The margin between success and failure often is surprisingly small. A Las Vegas game that regularly provides the casino with a 1 or 2 percent margin over costs will soon make the owners of the casino wealthy. Grocery stores that earn 2 percent profit on their gross sales ordinarily are quite successful, while those that only earn 1 percent profit on their sales struggle and often fail. On most football teams, coaches that consistently can win six of every ten games are likely to keep their jobs, while those that can win only five of every ten games are much more likely to get fired.

What does this have to do with entrepreneurial personalities? Many companies and organizations wish they could hire an entrepreneurial leader. This is because legions of firms badly need vibrant, transformational entrepreneurial leadership from their CEOs. Yet, who are the individuals who actually become entrepreneurial CEOs and what are their characteristics?

One of the problems in any search for a CEO or leader is that many candidates are highly skilled at "talking story" (a Hawaiian phrase that often connotes exaggeration) with respect to their own entrepreneurial abilities, but ultimately they don't walk their talk. They know the jargon, but ultimately shrink from their own words. After they have been appointed, many promising leaders turn out to be timid, transactional leaders whose entrepreneurial activities are minimal.

Hence, boards of directors have a strong interest in identifying those candidates for leadership who are truly entrepreneurial versus those who are not. Boards want to avoid putting round pegs into square holes and they don't want to appoint individuals who eventually will fail. Boards have the ability to increase their chances of a successful appointment of an entrepreneurial CEO if they know what characteristics tend to typify entrepreneurs.

With respect to individuals, some (perhaps many) would like to become entrepreneurs and want to know if they have what it takes. Those who speculate about becoming entrepreneurs need to know that their inherited genetic endowment has much to say about their probability of success. Yes, they can "go to school," or observe successful entrepreneurs in action. Both of these activities are helpful. However, the evidence is compelling that it is not knowledge of accounting principles per se that produces entrepreneurial success, or for that matter, an understanding of the best way to write a business plan, or to build a Web site. Instead, a collection of entrepreneurial personality traits is the key.

Let us not be misunderstood. Knowledge, observation, experience, and environment are helpful to entrepreneurs, and we will have more to say about these influences. In the last analysis, however, it is the presence or absence of distinctive personality traits, especially those relating to risk-taking, that tell the tale. Reality is that successful entrepreneurs frequently have never darkened the door of a college classroom and likewise have been ignorant of many financial and economic precepts. It is easy to produce anecdotes to support this generalization. Consider J.R. Simplot, the inventor of the frozen French fry. He dropped out of school in 1923 at age fourteen and started his own business, which morphed into a $3 billion operation, not the least because his company became the primary supplier of potatoes to McDonald's. Still, the evidence is far more than anecdotal. Shane (2008) has mined U.S. Census data and has found that educational attainment, per se, has little to do with whether an individual will become a business-founding entrepreneur.

At the end of the day, it is visionary, energetic, confident, extroverted, and creative individuals who are not afraid of change and relish risk-taking who are most likely to become entrepreneurs. This does not mean budding entrepreneurs cannot be financial ignoramuses or that a simpleton is likely to become a successful entrepreneur. It does mean that academic knowledge concerning entrepreneurship seldom is the factor that determines whether or not one becomes an entrepreneur.

Similarly, we are not arguing that culture is without influence on entrepreneurship. There are significant, observable differences in the rate of entrepreneurship among countries around the world that are not a function of levels of economic development. Inside the United States, Shane (2008) and others have analyzed the relatively lower rates of entrepreneurial activity of African-Americans compared to other ethnic groups. Therefore, cultural and ethnic differences do exist. However, culture usually is trumped by genes and inherited personality traits. That is, whatever the cultural or ethnic environment, some individuals are more likely to become entrepreneurs than others.

Our points, therefore, are neither that introverted, risk-averse individuals that lack self-confidence will never start their own businesses, nor that individuals from certain cultures or ethnic groups will never achieve entrepreneurial success. A wide range of individuals choose to start their own businesses. Because of their own skill, luck, or other factors, it is unquestionable that some become successful entrepreneurs. Nevertheless, the evidence on these matters is clear. Simply put, the odds are stacked against individuals with certain personality traits. Some people are born with personality traits that naturally equip them for entrepreneurial activity. Further, these traits are not easily taught or acquired. In the last analysis, these personality traits most often separate the sheep from the goats insofar as entrepreneurial leadership is concerned.

We recognize that the theses we have just offered tend to draw hisses and boos from certain quarters. One group of critics contends that virtually anyone in the United States can become a successful entrepreneur even though empirical evidence is quite the contrary (see Shane, 2008). These critics are taken by the notion that the traditional American Dream can be realized by anyone who is willing to work hard. And, needless to say, there is something to this. Social and economic mobility in the United States may have diminished, but opportunities remain robust, and the ability of a single determined individual to climb the ladder of success has not diminished substantially. Even so, this does not mean that business-founding entrepreneurship is the primary means for specific individuals to attain personal success. Instead, the route upward for many non-entrepreneurially inclined individuals may be an accounting degree, a career in the legal profession, or a position in public service. There are many roads to the top of the mountain, and entrepreneurship is only one of them. These alternative paths will best suit individuals who are not entrepreneurially inclined and whose personality traits make them shy away from the new, the unexpected, and the assumption of risk. We regard it as self-evident that those individuals who decide upon careers as elementary school teachers in a suburban location have different personality traits (and probably different genetic dispositions) than those who become hedge fund specialists.

Our theses also predictably draw flak from the educational community. Many individuals have an almost unshakable faith that education can cure nearly any malady and hence can deal with entrepreneurial shortcomings in individuals or groups. Variants of this notion—that one can be taught to be an entrepreneur—are especially prevalent on college campuses where business majors and MBA students study entrepreneurship. Yes, it's true that business majors are more likely to start a business than the typical college graduate, but candidates for business degrees are hardly a random selection of the American population. They are self-selected and hence more likely to possess the personality traits that lead to entrepreneurship. In any case, Shane (2008) reports that agriculture, architecture, and law students are even more likely to start their own businesses than business majors. The bottom line is that it is much easier to teach individuals how to read balance sheets, or to manipulate supply and demand curves, than it is to teach them to become someone who relishes risk-taking and new experiences.

We would ourselves be guilty of "talking story" if we now suggested that we have the ability to discern precisely who will be, or will not be, a successful entrepreneur. We cannot insure boards of directors against bad appointments or guarantee banks and investors that they will make wise investments in ventures that are proposed to them. But, both responsible bodies and individuals will reduce their errors if they understand better the genetic/environmental mix that generates entrepreneurial behavior and the human personality and life characteristics that tend to reflect entrepreneurial instincts. We also can help both boards and individuals to understand that it is difficult, though not impossible, to teach critical entrepreneurial personality traits that students acquire and actually apply.

The implications of these findings for business firms, universities, governmental agencies, the military, and foundations should not be overlooked. The best business schools in the world are predicated on the belief that many essential entrepreneurial traits can be learned, either in classrooms via instructions and case studies or by observing other entrepreneurs. The notion is that this learning can then be applied by students.

Business schools also believe that one can utilize a priori reasoning to illuminate behavior and forecast the future. For example, if vacationers drive their automobiles more miles each summer, then one can predict this will push up gasoline prices, unless other major influences intrude. There is nothing genetic about this theoretical conclusion, though it could be the case that the willingness of some individuals to act upon that prediction may be higher than that of others.

Would it be useful for an entrepreneur to be able to predict gasoline prices? Probably. But this will seldom be the critical factor that separates successful entrepreneurs from the rest.

The view that entrepreneurial traits can be inculcated successfully also is central to the efforts of the Kauffman Foundation, which is the most influential supporter of entrepreneurial research and instruction in the United States. While the Kauffman Foundation and business schools do not discount the role of heredity in generating and energizing entrepreneurs and founders, they believe that entrepreneurial attitudes and behavior usually can be productively analyzed and modified over time.

This is a reasonable, if not popular, point of view. However, Stevenson et al. (1999) report a National Federation of Independent Business (NFIB) study of 1,994 start-up businesses that discourages the notion that entrepreneurial risk-taking can be taught. The study found that "founders who spent a long time in study, reflection and planning were no more likely to survive their first three years than founders who seized opportunities that came by without much planning" (p. 19).

Business schools, governmental agencies, and the Kauffman Foundation cite numerous examples of businesses that have been turned around by the application of sound managerial principles and knowledge. This beneficent result appears particularly to hold true when the principles being learned are *inconsistent* with the unrehearsed intuition of CEOs and decision makers. That is, if the principles being learned lead to conclusions that executives did not already know intuitively, then these principles can be of greater use.

In the realm of economics and finance, for example, many CEOs may be unaware of the heavily documented tendencies of CEOs and investors to hold overly optimistic views about the future and to be very reluctant to acknowledge a loss (for example, refusing to sell a stock whose price has fallen, or declining to shut down a line of business that has failed). Thus, DeBondt and Thaler (1995) aver that "Perhaps the most robust finding in the psychology of judgment is that people are overconfident."

Consistent research and our own surveys reveal that most CEOs and entrepreneurs believe that it is *other* leaders who fall prey to such difficulties, not them. For example, a study of almost 3,000 entrepreneurs revealed that fully one-third of them believed their chances of success were 100 percent (Cooper, Woo, and Dunkelberg, 1988). In reality, about 75 percent of new businesses fail within five years.[2] Thus, as Stevenson et al. (1999) pithily put it, "The great majority of start-ups fold or drag along in what one entrepreneur calls the land of the living dead" (p. 18).

However, available data also suggest that a majority of all firm disappearances are voluntary (Cardozo and Borchert, 2003). Voluntary disappearances might occur because of sale or merger, but more likely reflect a business that is not doing well and the owner reading the handwriting on the wall. Once again, by most accountings, these latter might be regarded as business failures.

Similarly, both past research and our survey data indicate that while many CEOs talk boastfully about the risky decisions they make, a much smaller number actually choose to do so in meaningful situations and especially not where their own financial resources are at risk (MacCrimmon and Wehring, 1986).

Well-designed instruction can remedy misapprehensions such as these, though the evidence discourages the notion that teaching often actually alters CEOs' behavior. Our contention is not that business schools and the entrepreneurial efforts of the Kauffman Foundation are destined for failure, but instead that their efforts are much more likely to succeed if aimed at specific populations, namely, those individuals whose genetic makeup and personality traits predispose them to take advantage of such knowledge by acting in a truly entrepreneurial fashion. Just as a farmer who hopes to reap a healthy crop of wheat must sows seeds on fertile ground rather than rocks, those who seek to stimulate entrepreneurial activity must recognize that some individuals are much more inclined to act entrepreneurially than others.

Two individuals (Mary and Jane) who otherwise are identical in terms of cognitive ability, income, family backgrounds, education, and the like often react quite differently to entrepreneurial opportunities. Mary may relish risk-taking opportunities and an uncertain, but tantalizingly promising future, while Jane may shrink from such situations. This is a difficult, even confounding, notion for some individuals to accept because they perceive that it implies that education and training can't really reach some individuals effectively, at least where entrepreneurial attitudes and activities are concerned. Nevertheless, this is the implication of behavioral genetics research (which we will examine shortly) and our own survey evidence.

THRIVING IN AMBIGUITY

Almost fifty years ago, Daniel Ellsberg (1961), later to become famous for other reasons (the Pentagon Papers episode in 1971), provided strong evidence that most decision makers dislike ambiguity. They prefer certainty and situations where unexpected outcomes are rare. The difference between entrepreneurs and other individuals is that entrepreneurs usually thrive in ambiguous situations.

Our goal for this book is to increase the probabilities of success confronting entrepreneurs, boards of directors, and investors. One means to do this is to demonstrate what is *not* true (Popper, 1959). That is, in this book, we "falsify" some popularly held notions about entrepreneurs and entrepreneurship and show that while this may be the conventional wisdom, such notions are often invalid. Knowing what is not true often is as valuable as knowing what is true. It may be comfortable to assume that the principles of entrepreneurial success can both be taught to, and implemented by, nearly any intelligent, alert individual, but the available evidence discourages this notion.

The bottom line is that entrepreneurs are demonstrably different from other individuals and behave differently than non-entrepreneurial CEOs. Nevertheless, some are inclined to believe that successful entrepreneurs are ordinary individuals who simply have been the lucky recipients of fate. Figuratively, in this view, successful entrepreneurs are individuals who happen to be standing in a fortuitous location when a bolt of financial lightning strikes.

The perception that there's not much difference between those who are successful and those who fail perhaps motivated a famous retort by Ernest Hemingway. When F. Scott Fitzgerald casually observed, "The rich are very different from you and me," Hemingway dyspeptically responded, "Yes, they have more money," suggesting that they really aren't different.

Was Hemingway correct, at least where entrepreneurs are concerned? Is the only difference between successful entrepreneurs who have founded their own firms and other CEOs the size of their bank accounts and perhaps a bit of luck? While some individuals with egalitarian instincts might prefer to believe so—that entrepreneurs are no different than other individuals— the truth is otherwise. Entrepreneurs are profoundly different from other individuals and even from other CEOs who did not found their own firms. Some entrepreneurs may be wealthier than the rest of us[3] and some may be visibly lucky,[4] but as we shall see, those are not the major sources of the differences that exist between them and other individuals.

ENTREPRENEURSHIP ON DECLINE?

Shane (2008) reports that contrary to popular belief, entrepreneurship is on the decline in the United States and that numerous other countries are more entrepreneurial than the United States. He relies upon the proportion of individuals who start their own businesses as the primary basis for his conclusions. Shane also argues that media focus upon Silicon Valley entrepreneurs is misleading and unrepresentative of actual entrepreneurship in the United States, which is far more mundane. The typical entrepreneur, he says, is a married White man in his forties who may not have attended college and who starts a decidedly low-tech firm with $25,000 or less from his own savings.

Let us cast the issues in front of us in terms of dollars and cents. The value of the gross domestic product of the United States exceeded $14,080 billion ($14.080 trillion) in the fourth quarter of 2007 (BEA, 2008; annualized).

This is about $46,000 for every citizen. How we generate, expand, utilize, and manage this bounty must be regarded as a critical question in the twenty-first century. The United States boasts the most productive economy in the history of the world. Not just Americans, but all world citizens would be better off if we understood better the managerial and entrepreneurial parameters that have defined this splendid achievement.

HOW MUCH DOES LUCK COUNT?

Gompers, Kovner, Lerner, and Scharfstein (2006) examined the probability of success by several different kinds of entrepreneurs. Those who succeeded in a prior venture had a 30 percent chance of succeeding in a new venture, while first-time entrepreneurs succeeded only 18 percent of the time. Those who failed previously and tried again had a 20 percent chance of success in their new venture.

HOW OUR APPROACH DIFFERS

In August 2007, we searched Amazon.com for books relating to the term "entrepreneur" and were confronted with 92,181 choices. The word "entrepreneurial" produced 50,233 possibilities. In truth, the topic of entrepreneurship has been flogged to death by thousands of writers. The usual approach to entrepreneurial study is anecdotal. The author usually focuses on one or more entrepreneurs and implicitly invites us to assume that these individuals are representative. Or, if the author does not believe the targeted entrepreneur is representative, then that entrepreneur is held up as being especially interesting, an intriguing and semi-exotic species, or the leadership equivalent of a genetic aberration that is worthy of study in its own right.

Representative is Bo Peabody's *Lucky or Smart? Secrets to an Entrepreneurial Life* (2004), which contains the reminiscences and counsel of a still young entrepreneur who has started five companies. His story is remarkable, and Peabody truly is a very interesting character. And, we confess that we love great tales that chronicle the triumphs and defeats of leaders, whether in business, politics, academe, or sports. Shortly, we'll present another interesting and illuminating example below. Our purpose in this book, however, is to present *valid empirical generalizations* that can be made about large numbers of individuals who have founded their own firms. We then will compare these individuals to other CEOs who haven't founded the firm for which they work as well as to a large group of non-profit CEOs—college and university presidents—that we have studied previously. In this book, then, we are less concerned with the idiosyncratic characteristics of a single entrepreneur and more concerned with makeup of entrepreneurs, particularly founders, as a group.

A plenitude of anecdotal studies of entrepreneurs exists, and they are highly differentiated. The skillful telling of these stories oftentimes produces best sellers. Some are autobiographies reminiscent of after-the-battle books penned by military commanders who have surmounted the challenges of war and subsequently seek to share their absorbing experiences. Not so coincidentally, they seek to shape history to their own satisfaction.

Other autobiographies contain philippic passages in which the author attempts to even scores with various critics and tormentors. Whatever the intent, most of these books are ghosted by professional writers or written with extensive professional assistance. Nearly all offer alluring stories that purport to contain broad lessons for other leaders and entrepreneurs. Representative are Iacocca's 1984 rendition of his times at Ford and Chrysler, Sam Walton's 1993 portrait of the astounding growth of Wal-Mart, Michael Dell's instructive 1999 chronicle of the emergence of Dell as a "just in time" inventory, direct-to-consumer vendor, Gerstner's 2002 description of how IBM was turned around, and Welch's 2001 and 2005 descriptions of his flourishing run at General Electric and what he now perceives to be the secrets of winning.

One need not read these volumes intensively to deduce the critical factors that these CEOs believe made them and their firms successful. Their paths to success are hardly national security secrets and typically involve old-fashioned verities—hard work, perseverance, courage, loyalty, a willingness to take risks, the ability to prioritize, a finely honed ability to listen and communicate, a regard for employees and colleagues, and the like. To a person, each of these successful and sometimes eccentric CEOs radiated charisma, though the sources of their individual charisma were surprisingly variable. Taking a broad view, we can observe that few CEOs or CEO aspirants would go wrong if they were able to replicate such general talents and values in their own businesses. The problem, of course, is that every entrepreneurial situation is different and requires a distinctive approach that usually has precious little to do with General Electric or some other large corporation.

The admirable qualities (and their antitheses) cited in these anecdotal biographies are sufficiently generic that they usually do not provide much specific guidance to aspiring entrepreneurs and CEOs. When Sam Walton counsels the merits of a flat administrative structure and inveighs against excessive administrative salaries and perquisites, this is worthy advice, yet it does not always easily translate to idiosyncratic local situations.

For example, how much is too much flattening of the administrative hierarchy in a highly decentralized and regionalized industry such as milk production? Answers to questions such as this are not obvious. Hence, whether or not CEOs have read best sellers such as these, or even have read their own books, they often must make judgment calls based upon their intuition. Only later will they find out that their intuition served them for good or ill. Perhaps their intuition was based vicariously on Sam Walton's experiences, which may or may not have matched the local situation. In any case, Mr. Walton's advice is contradicted by other CEOs and even by empirical evidence generated by academics and analysts.

The most important insights in anecdotal CEO books have tended to be those relating to dynamic business processes that still are evolving and far from maturation. Corporations such as Wal-Mart and Dell have become leaders in transforming purchasing processes, inventory control, supply chain management, and pricing throughout the economy. We have not yet seen the last of these developments because many are intimately connected to globalization, which bodes only to increase. To be sure, no reader is going to learn supply chain management from Michael Dell's book, but she may well come to understand the central and evolving nature of supply chain management to medium and large-sized corporations.

Still, it remains true that most of the insights reported in anecdotal CEO books already were well known by the time the books appeared. This underlines a generic difficulty associated with books that expatiate about the successes of CEOs and firms. By the time the books are published, the information contained within them already has been widely circulated and heralded in outlets such as the *Wall Street Journal, Business Week, Forbes,* and *Fortune.* Those who can utilize such knowledge typically already possess it and have long since implemented it if they found it relevant. The function of anecdotal CEO books, then, is usually to provide a popularized, less technical, reader-friendly version of past events and trends. Contrary to the advertising bluster that often accompanies anecdotal CEO books, they should not be interpreted as handbooks for CEO success.

None of this suggests that laudatory anecdotal CEO books are not useful, for they can be helpful in providing lay people with a general sense of values, attitudes, processes, and decision-making milieu in the business world. Further, as Donald Trump can confirm, captivating stories can function as a device for advertising one's products, if not one's own person. Nevertheless, most readers rapidly encounter diminishing marginal utility with respect to works in this genre because, except for the local color and anecdotes, they've heard it all before, or the lessons are too general to be applicable to a particular situation.

Yet another class of books about CEOs is written about them rather than by them. Some of these contributions are undertaken with the direct permission and cooperation of the focal CEO and therefore tend to be hagiographic. In these publications, there is a tendency to view the world through rose-colored glasses. More entertaining (though not always more accurate) are studies of CEOs that are designed as exposés. These efforts can be mightily disheartening, unexpectedly titillating, or amenably comical, but typically are designed to generate outrage at the CEO and his practices. Included here are Byrne's 1999 look at Al "Chainsaw" Dunlap, whose forte was downsizing companies with a degree of haste and brutality, and Gasparino's *Blood on the Street* (2005), which examined how several of the largest and most influential Wall Street brokerage houses duped many thousands of investors. Such books ordinarily read like the script from an old 1940s western cowboy movie; the good guys and bad guys are easily identified.

The demise of Enron, Tyco, and WorldCom has produced a spate of additional books that reside firmly inside this tradition. Each of these revolves around the misdeeds of a particular CEO, and these transgressions are presented as a paradigm for the threatened existence or emergence of a darker, more dangerous business climate. Skillfully angering and alarming readers about exploding Pinto automobile gasoline tanks or poisoned apples frequently is a productive book sales technique and on occasion leads to legislation designed to correct the problem. In that sense, the revelatory disclosure CEO books exercise an anodyne function because they allow the reader to "solve" a problem or dilemma.

Exposé CEO stories often are riveting and nearly always evoke appropriate levels of disgust for the egregious indiscretions of the CEOs. If one is searching for the murky underside of American business, one need go no further than these books. Nevertheless, like the volumes written about and by the most successful CEOs, this genre does not readily yield to specific advice or knowledge for an aspiring CEO, unless one considers "don't steal from stockholders" and "don't cheat the IRS" to be situation specific. While it's true that these prescriptions are rather universal with respect to CEOs, one hopes that it is not necessary to purchase a book about the chicanery of Tyco in order to comprehend these things.

We believe that the progress of science frequently is a sequential process that begins with the generation of hypotheses with testable implications that may then be subjected to rigorous statistical tests to determine their predictive and explanatory validity. The hypotheses may be innovative and perhaps challenge convention. Some may yield predictions that are not immediately testable because of data limitations. Nonetheless, if these hypotheses can be tested empirically, we can improve our knowledge about how the world works. In our case, we want to know how CEOs behave, what they value and believe, and where this comes from. Such knowledge will better enable us to isolate the key aspects of reality with respect to CEOs and improve our ability to predict CEO success or failure.

AN EXEMPLARY FOUNDING ENTREPRENEUR

Having just proclaimed that anecdotal evidence seldom leads to the valid scientific generalizations we require, we now note that anecdotes sometimes can be helpful in clarifying the issues and in highlighting critical questions. For that reason, we present a brief description of an amazing entrepreneur who for the next paragraph will remain nameless.

He grew up in a government housing project in Washington, contracted polio when he was eight years old and spent six years in a hospital. After his parents divorced, he bounced around the West Coast, living with relatives. By age fourteen, he was self-sufficient. He graduated from high school in Missoula, Montana, while living with his grandmother and then went off to seek his fortune in Alaska. He worked on heavy construction there, learned the ropes, and then returned to Montana, where he founded his own company, starting with a single Caterpillar tractor. His first contract involved paving a parking lot in a visitor's center in Glacier National Park. Within twenty years, he was on *Forbes* magazine's list of the wealthiest people in the world.

Who is this inspiring man? He is Dennis Washington, the chairman of Washington Corporations based in Missoula. Appropriately, he has served as the president of the Horatio Alger Association, whose membership is limited to entrepreneurial individuals such as Dennis Washington who have set out on their own, conquered significant odds, and achieved significant success.

Dennis Washington didn't write dime novels in the fashion of the real Horatio Alger (1832–1899), but his story is quintessential "rags to riches" fare, involving a risk-taking, plucky, driven individual who had a vision and triumphed against the odds.[5] Today's Washington Corporation consists of more than a dozen firms involved in construction, mining, railroads, and shipping. It does work all over the world and is involved in the rebuilding of the Middle East.

Now, to the point of this anecdotal exercise. On the face of it, it is difficult to argue that the Dennis Washingtons of the world really aren't a bit different from most of the rest of us. There is something about people such as Dennis Washington that is unusual. Such individuals visibly possess different personality traits, values, propensities, and behaviors than most of the rest of us, and they even stand apart from the typical corporate CEO who has risen to the top through the ranks of his company. We will provide both scientific evidence and survey data to support this premise.

occur that will cause me suffering, harm, loss, or danger. Risk is ubiquitous in modern life. Everyone incurs risk on a daily basis, and sometimes that risk emanates from sources of which we are blissfully unaware. I may be ignorant of the risk attached to not ingesting sufficient selenium, an essential trace element. Without sufficient selenium, the cardiac muscles of my heart will deteriorate. However, I may also be unaware that ingesting too much selenium can be toxic and fatal. Still, these risks exist even if I don't know about them.

Some risks can be calculated precisely, as where I decide to bet that a head will appear when a fair coin is flipped (the probability of a head is 0.5). Other risk cannot be easily computed—we don't know the precise probability that a hurricane will strike tomorrow, or the probability that a terrorist attack against the White House will occur next year.

As Peter Bernstein (2007) has pointed out, for most of human history, the weather was the main source of economic risk. Today, however, the main source of economic risk is our own actions and the actions of others. The central premise of this book is that some individuals abhor risks and attempt to minimize them, while others are attracted by risky situations and thrive when confronted with uncertain circumstances. These individuals, we will demonstrate, tend to become entrepreneurs.

RISK-AVERSION AND ENTREPRENEURSHIP: DEMOGRAPHY

Let's begin with studies that have addressed the impact of a variety of factors upon risk-taking. Risk-taking is at the very center of entrepreneurial activity. Table 2.1 summarizes available evidence that relates risk-taking to demographic characteristics. The assumption throughout is that increased risk-aversion reduces entrepreneurial activity (holding other things constant), a presumption that underpins virtually all rigorous entrepreneurial research.

A word of caution. Note well that demographic characteristics are not personality traits. For example, when we report below that most studies indicate that risk-aversion rises with age, this says nothing specifically about entrepreneurial personality traits. It is true that personality traits relevant to entrepreneurial activity may change as an individual ages, but it is an unmerited logical leap to conclude that this means it is these very traits that are the cause of increased risk-aversion. Such a hypothesis may hold water, but the conclusion does not follow logically from

Chapter 2

The Scientific Evidence

New paradigms shock the existing paradigm, but still leave open questior
                                                                    —Thomas S. Kuhn, '

Successful entrepreneurs are not just braggarts. They are highly
people who quickly generate a tremendous number of ideas—so
others ridiculous.

                                                                    —John I

The older one gets, however, the more most of us concl
come into the world with fixed personalities that ar
specific home or school environmental influences.

OK, you say, I now understand that you cor
different animals. They're not the same as
genetic basis to some of their entrepreneu
up or shut up. Precisely what is the sci
conclusion?

A VERY SHORT PRIMER ON RISK

Before we plunge forward,
mean by "risk." I incur risk when th.

Table 2.1 The Relationship between Entrepreneurial Risk-Aversion and Selected Variables: A Summary

Variable	Impact on risk-aversion and entrepreneurial activity
As wealth increases	Risk-aversion increases at a decreasing rate at high levels of wealth
As income increases	Risk-aversion increases at a decreasing rate at high levels of income
As age increases	Risk-aversion increases
Women	More risk-averse than men
Men	Less risk-averse than women
As education increases	Mixed impact
Marital status when married	Risk-aversion increases
Number of children	No significant impact
Parental background	No significant impact
Occupation	Mixed impact
Self-employed	Risk-aversion decreases
African-American	Risk-aversion increases
Hispanic/Latino	Risk-aversion increases
Immigrant status	Risk-aversion decreases
Religion	Mixed impact

Notes: The table assumes that entrepreneurs are risk-takers and that factors that increase risk-aversion also reduce entrepreneurial behavior. Hundreds of studies exist that report on the relationship between demographic variables and risk-taking. This table reports the general directions of this research, but should not be interpreted to mean either that all studies have found these results, or that these findings are invariant with respect to time, situation, and culture, or the manner in which risk-related questions are asked. All of the indicated relationships are ceteris paribus—the other variables are held constant in a multivariate relationship in which the dependent variable is a measure of risk-aversion.

Several of the entries in Table 2.1 deserve discussion. First, wealth, income, age, female status, and being married tend to increase risk-aversion,[1] though there is some evidence that older investors (seventy years plus) are more easily led astray and are more likely to make impulsive decisions than they would have ten or twenty years earlier. Similarly, members of minority groups such as African-Americans tend to be more risk-averse, though this does not hold true for immigrants. The accumulated evidence with respect to the impact of education on risk-aversion is mixed, as we might add, it is with respect to the impact of additional education on entrepreneurial activity and personality traits. Factors such as parental background, number of children, and religious activity do not appear to be consistently related to risk-aversion.

BEHAVIORAL GENETICS AND ENTREPRENEURIAL ACTIVITY

If personalities are an important key to CEO behavior and performance, then where do those personalities come from and how are they formulated?

Nearly all theories of personality assert that heredity, environment, or a combination of the two are responsible for the major features of personality we observe (Pervin and John, 2001; Friedman and Schustack, 2002; Hergenhahn and Olson, 2002; Pervin, Cervone, and John, 2004). The debate over the relative importance of heredity versus environment is many centuries old and dates back to the thirteenth century. It was Francis Galton, however, whose 1874 book *English Men of Science: Their Nature and Nurture* first posited the "nature versus nurture" discussion in more modern, scientific terms. Galton asserted that "Nature is all that a man brings with himself into the world; nurture is every influence that affects him after his birth" (p. 12). Today, the controversy continues with the balance increasing in favor of nature as the primary influence on personality; the question then is not whether genes influence personality, but how much and in what manner (Canli, 2006).

For our purposes, we are concerned with the sources of entrepreneurial behavior and tendencies. Where do they come from? To what extent is nurture important? Are individuals born with entrepreneurial characteristics that cannot easily be duplicated? To what extent can entrepreneurship be learned? (Azar, 1997a, b).

Virtually no one argues that heredity is the only thing that matters in personality formulation. Equally, however, no seriously regarded scholar adopts the early behavioral position that operant conditioning can produce nearly any desired behavior or personality (Azar, 1997a, b). Consider the extremity of Watson's famous 1924 statement:

Give me a dozen healthy infants & my own specific world to bring them up in, & I'll guarantee to take any one at random & train him to become any type of specialist I might select—doctor, lawyer, artists, merchant chef & yes, even beggar & thief, regardless of his talents, penchants, tendencies, abilities, vocations, and race of his ancestors. (p. 82)

Even Watson modified his stance on this issue in later years and admitted to the role of heredity as a determinant of behavior, though he continued to believe that environment trumped heredity in terms of its relative importance.[2] Subsequent practitioners in this tradition such as B. F. Skinner (1974) saw personalities and behavior as being determined primarily by learning based upon consequences and reinforcement. Skinner believed that it was possible to modify and shape behavior by extinguishing undesirable behaviors (however defined) and replacing them with desirable behaviors. The primary means to accomplish this were reinforced consequences, positive and negative, that resulted in learning. Skinner, who engaged in extensive experimentation with both animals and humans, also argued that negative reinforcements do not work as well as positive reinforcements. However, empirical evidence suggests that failures teach more durable lessons than successes.

Disentangling the influences of heredity and environment is a very difficult process. The most common attempts to do so involve one of the following three strategies: (1) studies of biological twins; (2) studies of adopted children; and (3) gene identification. The twin and adoption studies are the most easily understood. In the words of McGue and Bouchard (1998), "The classical twin study involves the comparison of monozygotic and dyzygotic twins reared together (MZTs and DZTs). If genetic factors influence the trait in question, MZTs, who share 100% of their genetic material, should be more similar than DZTs, who, like ordinary siblings, share on average only 50% of their genetic material" (p. 3). One can also observe identical twins (MZTs) that have been reared separately to observe the impact of environment on individuals whose heredity is identical. In this latter case, it is heredity that is held constant, while environment is varied.

MONOZYGOTIC TWINS (MZ)

are identical twins born from the fertilization of a single egg. MZT twins are identical twins raised together, while MZA twins are identical twins raised apart.

DYZYGOTIC TWINS (DZ)

are fraternal twins born when a woman double ovulates and each egg is fertilized independently. MZT twins are fraternal twins raised together, while MZA twins are fraternal twins raised apart.

In the case of adopted children, their genetic material is different from other children in a family, but their environment is similar. In this case, it is environment that scientists attempt to hold constant, while heredity is varied. Unfortunately, there is strong evidence that parents do not treat their children the same, even when they are raising identical twins (Carey, 2003). Hence, this approach generates arguable results.

What do these studies tell us? Twin and adoption studies lead to the conclusion that most, if not all, behavioral characteristics are heritable. As Ridley (2003) put it, "The twin studies have caused a genuine revolution in the understanding of personality" (p. 82).

Note that "heritable" does not mean that any behavioral characteristics in question (for example, those associated with entrepreneurial activity) are exclusively determined by heredity, but rather that heredity has much to do with those personality traits. Heritability is seldom a pure measure of genetic inheritance because there is potential interaction between heredity and environment. Consider a pregnant mother who smokes heavily, or who receives a large dose of radiation. Such events will affect her children.

One of the most controversial conclusions of twin and adoption studies is that the most important environmental influences on behavior are those that are *not* shared by reared-together relatives (McGue and Bouchard, 1998; Bouchard et al., in DiLalla, 2003). This finding is counterintuitive, for it suggests that to the extent that environment matters, general familial environmental influences such as family stability, parental educational, and income levels, plus a variety of other advantages are much less important in determining behavior than environmental influences outside the family. This is a powerful inference because it asserts that the manner in which parents raise their children eventually won't make a significant difference in the personalities and intelligence of those children, especially as the children grow older and leave the family. While most of the twin and adoption studies point in this direction, few scientists hew to this line rigidly and even those who generally support this view agree that extreme cases of child abuse and neglect are likely to make a difference in children's personalities. That said, the importance of this research is that after one has taken heredity into account, home environment has much less to do with the subsequent intelligence, personalities, and happiness of children than most have previously believed.

As applied to entrepreneurs and founding CEOs, the twin and adoption studies point in the direction of entrepreneurs and founders being born, not made. At its extreme, this is a view of entrepreneurship and founding CEOs that conjures visions of Roy Hobbs, the extremely gifted baseball player in Bernard Malamud's 1952 novel, *The Natural*. Hobbs, who was played by Robert Redford in the eponymous movie, was so marvelously talented that he could dominate major league baseball pitching without coaching or any significant minor league experience. Nor did he even need to practice much to exercise his considerable physical gifts, though he had other failings that brought him low. Hobbs was "hardwired" genetically to be a superb baseball player.

In this view, you either have the talent to be a founding entrepreneur or you don't, and the necessary talents cannot easily be taught. This is an outlook diametrically opposed to the behaviorism of Watson and Skinner, as well as to the cultural determinism of famed anthropologist Margaret Mead (1928). Shortly, we will examine the inclinations of CEOs on these issues when we present our survey data. We hasten to note, however, that even though the views of CEOs are interesting because of the central roles they play in the entrepreneurial process, their opinions should not be confused with rigorous research.

In any case, the conclusions of the twin and adoption studies have drawn heavy intellectual comment and no little fire. Consider the contributions of Kagan (2000) and Kagan and Snidman (2004), who argue that heritability research doesn't really show what its strongest proponents believe it does. In particular, they argue that the many interactions between heredity and environment are neglected in most heritability estimating equations. They also assert that it is never possible actually to measure a person's environment. As illustration, they stress that it is incorrect to assume the environment of identical twins is the same even if they have been raised in the same home by the same parents. Differences, some large and others small, some random and others deliberate, always exist.

Kagan, who occupies an intermediate position in the heredity versus environment discussions because his research suggests that both matter, often relies upon examples from the animal kingdom to buttress his points. He notes that fruit flies with a specific genetic endowment usually develop abnormal wings, but this result occurs only when these flies are raised in a controlled situation where the temperature is about 20 degrees centigrade. However, if the ambient temperature is raised to 30 degrees centigrade, the fruit flies develop "almost normal wings" (Kagan, 1998). He interprets this to mean that small changes in environment often can elicit major changes in physical characteristics that are usually thought to be hereditary.

Nor is the evidence on the interaction between heredity and environment limited to fruit flies. Two Spanish scientists, Fraga and Esteller (Weiss, 2005), have provided provocative though still preliminary evidence that environmental influences such as eating patterns, pollutants, and even powerful emotional experiences can influence gene activity. This new field of research has been labeled as epigenetics and asserts that environmental influences will turn some genes "on" and other genes "off," and this "on/off" process varies during a person's lifetime, for example, during puberty and menopause. Thus, even identical twins gradually assume different genetic identities over time because of environmental factors, some of which are random. As a consequence, one twin may become more susceptible to cancer than another, or one may develop a different personality than the other.[3]

Thus, most genetic scientists today believe that environment can influence heredity and therefore it is not nearly as easy to separate the influences of heredity and environment from each other as many formerly assumed. The upshot is that while the accumulated evidence strongly suggests that some individuals are born with entrepreneurial personality inclinations, it may also be possible that the genes responsible for such entrepreneurship may be switched off as those individuals' lives progress. On the other hand, it also may be possible that on/off gene activations may enable other individuals to acquire entrepreneurial characteristics later in life.

Therefore, it appears that the interaction between nature (heredity) and nurture (environment) is a dynamic process that continues throughout most individuals' lives. Nevertheless, whether our focus is musical talent, natural athletic ability, or entrepreneurial personality instincts, we can observe that it is better to be born with such genes present and turned on as opposed to hoping that one's environment will come to one's rescue later in life.

Behavioral genetic research supports the notion that some aspects of behavior do appear to have hardwired origins and this becomes evident at an early age. The amygdala portion of the brain of certain individuals is much more active than that of others when these individuals are confronted with novel or unanticipated circumstances (again, see among many, Kagan and Snidman, 2004; Herrington et al., in Canli, 2006). Individuals who thrive when confronted with novelty or unanticipated circumstances are much more likely to become entrepreneurs than others. Since the "thriving on novelty" personality quality has a strong genetic component, this has led researchers to the conclusion that there is substantial heritability associated with entrepreneurial activities, including critical risk-taking behavior. But we must be measured here. Heritability does not rigidly determine either personality traits or aspects of personality such as entrepreneurial activity (Ridley, 1999). Instead, heritability constrains, guides, and molds the probability distribution of outcomes. Individuals with certain genetic endowments simply are much more likely than others to become entrepreneurs.

Over the past two decades, research on personalities most often has been conducted inside a model that in shorthand has become known as the "Big Five."

The five factors are as follows:

- Extroversion
- Agreeableness
- Conscientiousness
- Neuroticism and emotional stability
- Openness to experience and ideas

The first and fifth factors are most relevant to our concerns although each of the other three factors has something to do with entrepreneurial tendencies and success. While there are exceptions, most entrepreneurs tend to extroversion and must be open to new ideas and approaches if they are to succeed. Loehlin (1992) and Bouchard (1994, 1998) have found that there is statistically significant heritability associated with all of the Big Five personality factors, including openness to new experiences and ideas. Heritability, however, accounts only for about one-half of the observed "openness" personality trait, leaving one to conclude that environment (including random influences) might be responsible for the remainder (Carey, 2003).

Cloninger, Svrakic, and Przybeck (1993) examined what we previously termed the "novelty seeking trait" in individuals. Those individuals who possess this trait are more likely to explore the unknown and take changes, but also are more impulsive and excitable. Subsequent research typically though not always has found connections between this personality trait and body chemistry in the form of hormonal secretions, one of which is dopamine, which acts in the fashion of a medication that increases heart rate and blood pressure (Ebstein et al., 1996; Benjamin et al., 1996; Kluger, Siegfried, and Ebstein, 2002). The direct implication is that there are chemical differences between individuals that are highly entrepreneurial and those who are more rigid and reflective, and these chemical differences are substantially heritable.

Sam Calgione, who founded the innovative and successful Dogfish Head microbrewery, aptly described the sometimes rapturous feeling that accompanied his entrepreneurial activities: "An entrepreneur who witnesses a vision come true and sees the reflection of that vision in the eyes of customers and coworkers is participating in the development of a magical, culture-transforming entity" (Calgione, 2005, p. 18). Brewmaster Calgione may not have been conscious of the surge of his hormones at such times, but behavioral genetics research tells us that this is what was happening.

Research also has pointed strongly to the heritability of non–Big Five personality traits, including memory and one's desire or ability to remember details. Scarr and Weinberg (1981) and Bouchard et al. (2003), for example, found that a measure of authoritarianism in personalities was substantially heritable. The latter researchers also found that conservatism was strongly influenced by genetic factors and, to the surprise of many, that religiousness also exhibited heritability in their twin studies.

These findings may or may not be relevant to founding CEOs, depending upon one's view of the world. Are founding entrepreneurs more or less authoritarian, conservative, or religious than the rest of the population? The largely anecdotal literature on the subject contains contradictory examples, and there has been no rigorous study of these factors as they might apply to entrepreneurs. The survey data we will shortly present suggest that entrepreneurs are a bit more authoritarian, politically more conservative, and more religious than other CEOs. These are interesting findings, though once again we must stress that their views will not necessarily tell us what is actually true.

Finally, it is a reflection of the parochialism of academic disciplines today that a recent scholarly book summarizing the state of entrepreneurial research (Alvarez, Agarwal, and Sorensen, 2005) contains virtually nothing relating to the evidence we have presented in this section. Behavioral genetics research is ignored in the book, and the influence of heredity upon entrepreneurship is shunted aside despite its claim to focus upon interdisciplinary perspectives. This is unfortunate, for it sends a message how far off the mark much of our modern entrepreneurial research is. If nothing else, the narrowness of this coverage provides a persuasive argument for explicating the issues and publishing of this book.

NON-BEHAVIORAL GENETICS EVIDENCE

We've already noted that many CEOs talk more about risk-taking than actually doing it. Nevertheless, the weight of previous studies indicates that entrepreneurs who have founded their own firm take more risks than ordinary CEOs, whom we might label "managers" (Brockhaus, 1980). More recently, Chen, Greene, and Crick (1998) concluded that CEOs who had founded their own firms exhibited a propensity to take risks far beyond that of the CEOs we have labeled managers. A 2001 review of the literature by Stewart and Roth reached a similar conclusion.

There are at least two reasons why entrepreneurs might have a greater inclination to take risks. The first reason is situational. For whatever reasons, entrepreneurs find themselves in circumstances that require risk-taking and they react accordingly. Second, however, their very presence in risk-taking situations may be at least partially the product of self-selection. That is, individuals who are inclined to take risks gravitate to entrepreneurial situations because it is there that they are able to exercise their risk-taking preferences. Georges Doriot, the founder of the first significant venture capital company in the United States (American Research and Development Corporation), thrived on risky ventures and made his living investing in proposals that caused conventional banks to thumb their noses. Samuel Insull literally bet his life in 1903 on whether a new turbine electric generator, the world's largest, he had developed would work as he predicted rather than explode (Evans, 2004). It did not explode and he became a rich and influential man.

Thus, it seems likely that individuals who are hardwired genetically to exhibit personality characteristics associated with entrepreneurial activity will be among those who self-select by starting their own firm or by engaging in similar entrepreneurial activity. Curiously, in this regard, entrepreneurs bear some resemblance to criminals who are attracted by the prospect of risky though ill-gotten gains. Most criminals are not risk-averse, and neither are entrepreneurs. A quick caveat—no, we're not contending that most entrepreneurs are criminals, or vice versa, but it remains true that there is some overlap in their personality characteristics.[4]

Research on founding entrepreneurs has found that on occasion they are capable of tolerating "extreme resource deprivation" (Hoang and Gimeno, 2007, p. 3); many have become accustomed to negative feedback, much of which they block out or choose to ignore (Gatewood, Shaver, and Gartner, 1995); and, some are maladjusted socially and do not maintain significant conventional social relationships (Lee and Tsang, 2001). Yes, it is fair to conclude that some entrepreneurs are highly distinctive individuals that some regard as misfits even while others find them refreshing deviations from the stultifying mean.

The popular media have consistently cultivated and popularized an image of entrepreneurs that suggests they possess personalities significantly different from other individuals. Popular movies such as *Back to the Future* (with its friendly, hair askew, but slightly mad scientist-inventor played by Christopher Lloyd) propagate this image. Entrepreneurs in literature frequently are painted as being "a bit odd" or even "a bit crazy," though perhaps what is really meant is that they are different. Of course, it is not as if there isn't some empirical evidence in favor of such portrayals; more than a few entrepreneurs do not seem to fall smoothly into society's conventional slots. However, the research findings that encourage these conclusions usually apply to a few entrepreneurs, most especially to highly successful entrepreneurs, and not necessarily to all entrepreneurs as a group.

An interesting strain within this work is the view of some sociologists that many entrepreneurs are losers and misfits (Min, 1984, provides a survey of the evidence that now is a bit dated). Sandage's *Born Losers: A History of Failure in America* (2005) provides a delightful panoply of examples of unsuccessful entrepreneurs, but does not directly address the question of whether failure often is a prerequisite to success.

Even so, a word of caution is merited. We should remember that the typical entrepreneur in the American economy is a married white man in his forties who leads what many might regard as a pedestrian life (Shane, 2008). Despite this, the media tend to focus on individuals who turn out to be unusual even in an entrepreneurial context—highly successful people such as Bill Gates, Meg Whitman, or even "The Donald," Donald Trump. However, the typical entrepreneur invests less than $25,000 (mostly from her own savings) in a low-tech initiative that eventually fails. These individuals found corner grocery stores, dry-cleaning establishments, lawn-care operations, and restaurants. However, they have little sex appeal to the media, who prefer to focus on the very few entrepreneurs who become millionaires or who are newsworthy oddballs. And there's no denying that the saga of Sergey Brin and Larry Page starting Google in a garage in Menlo Park, California, is more interesting to most people than the story of a Korean immigrant green grocer opening a destined-to-fail store on the west side of Chicago.

In fact, both economic reversals and success are conducive to self-employment and entrepreneurship (witness An Wang of Wang Laboratories, who experienced both highs and lows, usually the result of his own decisions). However, those in the vast middle of income and asset distributions, where both conspicuous failure and success are absent, are, comparatively speaking, less likely to become entrepreneurs.

Does wealth make a difference? The answer is yes, if the question is, do wealth and the availability of capital increase the likelihood that someone will become an entrepreneur? (Blanchflower and Oswald, 1998). Nevertheless, if the question is whether individuals with substantial assets possess greater entrepreneurial abilities, then the answer is no (Evans and Jovanovic, 1989). What wealthy people, including those who have inherited money, have is more capital. Not surprisingly, this enables them to undertake entrepreneurial activities, but this does not translate per se to greater entrepreneurial abilities.

In fact, the easy availability of funds often is associated with poor entrepreneurial decision making. Roger Smith and John DeLorean in the automobile industry fall into this category, both having consistently underestimated the obstacles they faced and perhaps assuming their own decision-making invincibility as well. More recently, Dennis Kozlowski of Tyco, who now resides in a federal penitentiary, became famous for appearing to know all the answers, even to questions that had not been asked. He also famously blurred the boundaries between his firm and his own personal interests.

Evans and Leighton (1989) studied cohort of 4,000 white men who were tracked between 1966 and 1981 as a part of the *National Longitudinal Survey of Young Men*. The pair utilized a Rotter Scale score for each of their 4,000 individuals as a predictive variable. A Rotter Scale attempts to measure an individual's locus of internal control, that is, the extent to which a person believes that she determines her own success and controls her own performance. Evans and Leighton found that individuals with high Rotter Scale scores (reflecting a belief that they control their own destinies) were more likely to become entrepreneurs and start their own business (again, other things held constant). This is not genetic evidence, but behavioral genetics would regard it as a manifestation of the differing genetic endowments of individuals.

Many modern entrepreneurial studies are built on McClelland's 1961 theory of entrepreneurship that places primary emphasis on the personality needs of entrepreneurs. McClelland argued that entrepreneurs feel an urge to build products, processes, ideas, and firms, but interestingly hypothesized that they are only moderate risk-takers. Several studies of entrepreneurial personalities have built on McClelland's basic model. Collins and Moore (1970) examined more than 100 entrepreneurs and concluded they were strongly driven individuals who valued their independence. Bianchi's 1993 survey concluded that successful entrepreneurs were more likely to (1) have parents who were self-employed, (2) have been fired from a job in the past, (3) be an immigrant, (4) have been employed in the past by a large firm, (5) be the oldest child in their family, and (6) be a college graduate. Timmons' 1994 review of more than fifty studies identified six personality characteristics common among entrepreneurs (for example, commitment and determination, leadership, etc.). Licht (2007) similarly uncovered many dozens of studies that have typed entrepreneurs as being open to change, desiring to be their own boss, having high needs for achievement, and the like. Licht also argues that entrepreneurs "arguably excel in cross-linking and rearranging information in ways that lead them to new projects" (p. 831).

Blanchflower and Oswald (1998) quote a raft of studies, including their own, indicating that large numbers of individuals would like to become entrepreneurs and that those who have done so report substantially more happy lives than those who haven't. This is despite the fact that the average entrepreneur does not earn as much as the average salaried person (Hamilton, 2000). This is casual empirical evidence in favor of the "entrepreneurs are distinctive" hypothesis because it reveals that entrepreneurs willingly accept lower incomes in order to be their own bosses and assume the risks incumbent with going out on their own.

Miner's 1996a study of 100 established CEOs (forty-nine had founded their own firm and twelve were women) over a period of seven years led him to conclude that the "personality characteristics of entrepreneurs . . . are effective predictors of the subsequent success (growth) attained by the firms of these entrepreneurs" (p. 63). Using forty-three different test measures from seventeen psychological tests, Miner identified four personality types that he said led to entrepreneurial success: (1) personal achievers, (2) real managers, (3) empathetic super salespeople, and (4) expert idea generators. The more of these personality characteristics that are present in an individual, the more likely Miner said he was to be a successful entrepreneur. Miner's work, however, was dependent upon simple correlations between the entrepreneurs' test scores and their entrepreneurial activity.

Miner, who has spent much valuable time following and interviewing entrepreneurs, also briefly examined the profitability of the CEOs' companies along with their incomes (1997b), but did not actually hold all necessary variables constant in his empirical work. That is, he utilized simple two-variable correlations, which oftentimes can be deceptive. Profitability is the function of many different influences.

The fact that two variables are highly correlated (move together) does not mean one is the cause of the other. By way of illustration, there is almost a perfect positive correlation between fire departments and the appearance of fires. But, this does not mean that fire departments cause the fires. The direction of causation is reversed.

Similarly, while Miner related the age, education, gender, and ethnic background of the CEOs to entrepreneurial activity, these were not held constant either. Thus, it is not clear precisely what his interesting results signify.

Lee and Tsang (2001) investigated the effects of entrepreneurial personalities upon entrepreneurial success among 168 Chinese entrepreneurs in Singapore. Those who had a strong locus of internal control (and hence believed that they controlled their own futures) and those who had very strong needs for achievement were more successful. Those who were strongly self-reliant or extroverted were less successful. These are intriguing findings, for they suggest that successful entrepreneurs must believe they control their own destinies, but at the same time do not become too self-reliant. The ability to seek and accept the help and assistance of others at appropriate times, then, is a key to success, a finding replicated by Littunen (2000) and others. Nevertheless, the most important explanatory variable for entrepreneurial success was the entrepreneur's experience, including past experience that involved failures. All of these findings provide interesting evidence with respect to entrepreneurial personalities and are testable hypotheses within our own survey data set.

Entrepreneurs, then, have different personalities. Literally hundreds of studies support this generalization. Yet, to say that entrepreneurs are different does not address the central question—what's the source of this difference? The behavioral genetics research we surveyed earlier in this chapter supplies at least a partial answer. Many of the sources of the crucial personality differences between entrepreneurs and others are inherited rather than learned. That is, entrepreneurs tend to be born, not made.

INVENTION IS NOT INNOVATION

What do entrepreneurs do? They may invent, but they always innovate. Consider the example of John Pemberton, a Confederate Civil War veteran, who settled in Atlanta, opened a pharmacy and developed (invented) a syrup for a soft drink that later was christened Coca-Cola. Unfortunately, by 1886, the average sales of Coca-Cola were only thirteen drinks per day and so in 1888 Pemberton sold his rights to his invention for $2,300. It took John Biedenharn's business acumen in the 1890s (as well as his strategic decision to combine the syrup with carbonated water) before Coca-Cola would prosper. Biedenharn fortuitously possessed the entrepreneurial instincts and personality traits necessary to make something of Pemberton's discovery. He was an innovator.

The Coca-Cola example underlines the difference between invention and innovation. Inventors discover new knowledge; innovators apply that knowledge and produce new products. Sometimes those who invent also are those who capitalize upon their newly discovered knowledge and innovate. Edwin Land both invented the Polaroid camera process and developed it as a usable, salable product.

Nevertheless, it comes as a surprise to some when they learn that a clear majority of inventors are not innovators. Alexander Fleming invented penicillin in 1928, but others developed it and marketed it. Robert Watson Watt invented radar, but it was primarily Americans during and after World War II who developed this knowledge.

At the other end of the spectrum, Samuel Morse of telegraph fame really didn't invent anything; he was an entrepreneur who utilized others' discoveries. Bill Gates of Microsoft falls into the same category; neither he nor Microsoft ordinarily has been first to the market with new inventions, or even clever new innovations based on someone else's inventions. Microsoft's approach, whether intentional or not, has been to observe what works in the realm of software and the Internet and subsequently co-opt the original developer, usually by incorporating the new developments into Microsoft Windows or Microsoft Office. Spreadsheets, browsers, encyclopedias, search engines, and the use of a computer mouse all fall into this category.

The import of the inventor/innovator distinction for us is straightforward—the massive majority of entrepreneurs are innovators, not inventors. Entrepreneurs often develop new products and processes, but typically do so by relying upon already existing knowledge and well-known principles. What entrepreneurs bring to the party seldom is personal scientific brilliance, but rather a vision, energy, and the willingness to take risks. Edwin Drake did not discover oil or much of anything else, but he did figure out how to extract previously inaccessible oil (in Titusville, Pennsylvania in 1859) and this set off an economic boom (Evans, 2004). Drake presents an instructive example because his major supporter had sent him a letter withdrawing his financial support because he thought Drake's oil pumping efforts had come to naught. But the letter did not arrive until after Drake had hit pay dirt.

Similar to many entrepreneurs, Edwin Drake took major risks, many of which were financed with other people's money. But he was not an inventor in the usual sense because he relied upon off-the-shelf technology that he found ways to utilize in a novel fashion. But, there were disbelievers and agnostics with respect to Drake's work, and Evans (2004) reports that he was often called "Crazy Drake" (p. 120). Four of Drake's conspicuous characteristics—innovating rather than inventing, using other people's money, taking risks, and swimming against the tide—always have typified a very large proportion of entrepreneurs.

OUR SURVEY DATA

Our survey research was funded by the Kauffman Foundation, the premier supporter of research and teaching about entrepreneurship in the United States. Utilizing a tested and highly detailed survey instrument, and coupling this with measures of actual CEO and firm performance, we examined 234 entrepreneurs, 102 of which were founders of their firms. The 132 non-founders provide a robust CEO representative control group against which the founders can be measured. Appendix A provides a copy of the survey instrument.

Each participant in the survey supplied approximately 300 different pieces of information to us about their backgrounds, habits, and attitudes. *The data represent the most extensive, rigorously generated assemblage of information about the characteristics of individual entrepreneurs yet produced.* In spite of countless books and articles about entrepreneurs, there have been few statistically sound large sample studies that have focused on aspects of the entrepreneurial personality—attitudes, values, inclinations, beliefs, habits, approaches to problems, family and marital characteristics, politics and religious practices, and the like. In some cases, our findings may startle you, the reader. Nevertheless, we hope you will not only be intrigued, but also see the need for additional studies in this vein.

Have our survey respondents (a half dozen of which were CEOs of firms within *Fortune*'s 500) told us the truth about their backgrounds and what they really think? Honestly, we must say that even though each respondent was guaranteed complete anonymity, and this promise has been scrupulously honored, we cannot stipulate that we have captured precisely the accurate picture of these CEOs. Survey respondents sometimes have a tendency to choose replies that present themselves as they would like to be perceived rather than the way they actually are. Readers should keep this possibility in mind.

A NOTE ON SOURCE OF EVIDENCE

What sources of evidence are most reliable? The best evidence concerning entrepreneurial tendencies and activities emanates from behavioral genetics research because these studies can be replicated, checked, and used to formulate plausible hypotheses and generalizations. The second best evidentiary source is broad-based survey information generated by well-designed survey instruments such as we have utilized as a part of our Kauffman Foundation research. The least reliable evidence from the standpoint of one's ability to extrapolate from it is the anecdotal study that heretofore has dominated the study of entrepreneurial activity. Ironically, anecdotal studies may be the most interesting, but they seldom lead to useful generalizations and oftentimes are apologias that remind one of the self-justifying memoirs that generals and admirals write at war's end.

PERENNIAL WAVES OF CREATIVE DESTRUCTION

In 1923, famed Harvard economic historian Joseph Schumpeter described the unending waves of "creative destruction" of firms in the American economy that cause firms to appear and disappear. He viewed this entrepreneurial process as natural and endemic to capitalism. Schumpeter's creative destruction has accelerated eighty-five years later. In 2005, an estimated 671,800 new firms were created nationally and 544,800 disappeared (Small Business Administration, 2007). An average of 0.29 percent of all adults created a new business each *month* in 2006 (Fairlie, 2007). Interesting variations exist:

Men	0.35 percent
Women	0.23 percent
African-American	0.22 percent
Latino	0.33 percent
Asian	0.32 percent
Immigrant	0.37 percent
Less than HS education	0.36 percent
Montana	0.60 percent
Pennsylvania	0.17 percent

SUMMARIZING THE EVIDENCE

Scores of studies exist about entrepreneurs. At the end of the day, what do they tell us? Gartner (2005), a professor of psychiatry at Johns Hopkins, citing behavioral genetics evidence, has put forward a common though not universally accepted view of entrepreneurial personality, which we believe nonetheless aptly expresses the current state of opinion in the area:

Entrepreneurs... are often arrogant, provocative, unconventional, and unpredictable. They are not "well adjusted" by ordinary standards. Their stories can be inspiring, comical, sometimes tragic, and the hubris that fuels their improbable rise sometimes leads to their fall as well. Yet without their irrational confidence, ambitious vision, and unstoppable zeal, these outrageous captains would never have sailed into unknown waters, never discovered new worlds, and never have changed the course of our history. (p. 19)

The available behavioral genetics scientific evidence encourages this interpretation and the nonbehavioral genetic studies we have just reviewed are similarly supportive. As we shall see, our survey data also encourage this view. Yes, we believe the available evidence confirms our point of view. Yet, there are other, diametrically opposed views on the subject. Krueger (2007), for example, forthrightly opines that, " . . . experts, including entrepreneurs, are definitely made, not born" and cites the views of psychologists, sociologists, and human development theorists. The views of Shefsky (1994) are manifested in the title of his book, *Entrepreneurs Are Made, Not Born*. Critically, however, neither Krueger nor Shefsky provides any evidence from the realm of behavioral genetics. Both rely upon anecdotes as opposed to large-sample statistical evidence. Their work is in the normative spirit of McClelland (1961), whose work heretofore has guided so much of the analysis of entrepreneurship. This general approach ignores recent scientific advances, especially in behavioral genetics, and therefore has limited usefulness.

On the other hand, following Popper, it is possible to observe that the evidence already available now falsifies several popularly held views concerning entrepreneurial activity.[5] It simply is not true that all entrepreneurial activity is dictated by the entrepreneur's environment. Instead, there is a strong genetic component to both entrepreneurial activity and success. Similarly, the oft-held belief that certain key entrepreneurial personality traits such as extroversion and conservatism cannot be inherited is false. Every significant human personality trait appears to have some genetic basis, and therefore Krueger's assertions are extreme and represent a throwback to early behaviorists such as Skinner and Watson.

Thus, to return to a telling phrase, entrepreneurs are a different breed. They possess distinctive personalities, attitudes, values, and habits. The additional evidence we present in succeeding chapters provides strong support for this notion.

Chapter 3

Risk-Takers and Change Agents

We are all gamblers. And, as long as chance and uncertainty persist as features of human existence, we will continue to do so.
—Gerda Ruth, *The Age of Chance*, 1999

Ex ungue leonem. ("From a sample one can judge the whole.")
—Latin Proverb

Fools must be rejected not by arguments, but by facts.
—Flavius Josephus, Roman Governor of Galilee, c. 37–105

The essence of entrepreneurial behavior is risk-taking. Entrepreneurs may risk money, their reputations, or even their lives. If they're clever and "*can charm the birds out of the trees*" (the description of one of the entrepreneurs in our study by an angel venture capitalist), then they may find ways to risk someone else's money, reputations, or lives. Regardless, to some extent, all entrepreneurs are change agents because they intend to disrupt the status quo with new ideas, processes, and products.

The objectives of some entrepreneurs are relatively benign. One may wish no more than to establish a viable dry-cleaning outlet in a large city, while another's vision may not extend beyond adding fried chicken and pizza to the existing menu of sandwiches in her store.

Not infrequently, individuals may have no intent to become entrepreneurs, but their own use of a product stimulates their entrepreneurial glands. Stanford graduate students David Filo and Jerry Yang used the Internet in its early days and encountered problems keeping track of sites they had visited and the ones they really liked. They put their heads together and in 1994 developed what they then called "Jerry & David's Guide to the World Wide Web"—later to become the Internet giant Yahoo!

In all of these cases, however, there is a common thread. To some extent, all of these entrepreneurs placed themselves at risk. They invested their time or money to bring their promising ideas to fruition. Their initial aim may not be the creation of a company and may extend no further than wanting to make their own lives a bit easier. Witness mothers who largely on their own developed innovations such as folding car seats, jogging strollers, and a dozen other helpful devices that later became highly marketable (Shah and Tripsas, 2007).

By contrast, some entrepreneurs legitimately qualify as revolutionaries, for they intend to overthrow the existing economic state of affairs in their industry or market. Consider Niklas Zennström and Janus Friis, the inventors of Skype, the software program that enables computer users to make long-distance telephone calls to other Skype users anywhere in the world without charge. If E-Bay (which purchased Skype in 2005 for $2.76 billion) succeeds, then it will push conventional telephone companies out of the long-distance telephone business. Who could ever have predicted that two young Scandinavian Internet buffs could develop a freeware product that would have the potential to bring major international corporations to their knees?

NIKLAS ZENNSTRÖM AND JANUS FRIIS ARE NOT AMATEUR ENTREPRENEURS

In 2000, the founders of Skype developed *Kazaa*, a peer-to-peer file-sharing software package and system. Millions of individuals have utilized *Kazaa* to share music (illegally, according to music producers and artists). More recently, they have developed *Joost*, a system for distributing TV shows and other forms of video over the Web using peer-to-peer technologies.

Being first to the mark often is important for entrepreneurs, as Zennström and Friis's development of Skype confirms. The first firm to market an innovation often gains valuable market share, begins to enjoy economies of scale in its operations, and may establish standards that endure long thereafter, even if they are not the most efficient standards.

Further, particularly promising first-to-the-mark developments often become enticing to already established firms, which offer to purchase them (as E-Bay did in the case of Skype).

Even so, some entrepreneurs thrive by being second. They learn from the costly mistakes of original innovators and have the potential to jump into the market with a superior product at a lower cost. When the transformational promise associated with the Internet became obvious in the 1990s, Bill Gates realized that this historic development was largely bypassing Microsoft. He realized his firm was in danger of becoming the twenty-first century equivalent of an early twentieth century buggy whip manufacturer. Microsoft, he understood, needed to make a dramatic turnabout and cast off in new directions, lest it be pushed to the economic curb. This not only required a new corporate vision involving the Internet, but also the investment of tens of billions of dollars within a few years. It would cause severe disruption inside the firm and threaten the domains of a variety of individuals. Could Microsoft do it? Many doubted the giant's ability to turn on a dime.

Bill Gates and Microsoft became big-time risk-takers. Late to the Internet dance, they understood the corporation would be in jeopardy in just a few years if it did not transform itself and exploit the Internet successfully. The massive reallocation of Microsoft's attention and resources that resulted represents one of the biggest financial gambles in the history of American capitalism.

Yes, Microsoft owned a big bank account and Bill Gates was unlikely to go to the poor house if Microsoft ultimately did not succeed. And it's also true that Microsoft reduced a portion of its risks by hewing to its traditional policy of imitating the successes of other already established firms. If a competitor developed a successful Web browser (Netscape), an online encyclopedia (Britannica), or an audio and video player (Real), Microsoft followed suit and bundled its own often initially inferior version of these innovations into its Windows operating system. Subsequent versions of Windows offered steady and visible improvements to its sometimes mediocre initial efforts.

Some argue that Brobdingnagian Microsoft never really has succeeded in its quest to come to terms with the Internet and that more agile firms such as Google are in the process of eating its lunch. Perhaps. The reality, however, is that a decade later, Microsoft has sales approaching $45 billion annually and profits exceeding $12 billion annually.[1] Yet, it very well could have turned out differently.

The lesson we should draw from this episode has little to do with Microsoft's success and much more to do with the risks it assumed when it attempted to change directions. Risky ventures would not actually be risky if they always turned out to be successful. When entrepreneurs pursue their visions and take risks, they often fail, and Microsoft has recorded more than a few failures. Even the brilliant Thomas Edison sometimes whiffed as an inventor and entrepreneur. Edison missed the boat by failing to see the superiority of alternating electric current over his favored direct current.

On the other hand, in 1955 when Ray Kroc stopped selling milkshake mixer machines and decided to partner in the restaurant business with the McDonald brothers, he did magnificently well. But even he could not have anticipated that his budding firm would be serving 54 million customers per day in 120 countries by 2007.[2] Kroc took the fast-food hamburger plunge and succeeded beyond his wildest imagination.

The Ray Kroc/McDonald's story is one of legend. Yet, it should not divert us from the critical recognition that failure is part and parcel of entrepreneurial ventures. One reputable study found that 59 percent of all new restaurants opened in the late 1990s went out of business within three years.[3]

Did this staggering restaurant failure rate discourage enthusiastic prospective restaurateurs? Apparently not. RestaurantOwner.com reports that approximately 5,000 new restaurants open each month in the United States. Some may be pedestrian ventures that will increase the sales of Pepto-Bismol, while others may incorporate visionary nouvelle cuisine and unusual milieus. The common thread, however, is the assumption of risk by an entrepreneur, hopes of success, and the possibility of failure. It is not necessary to risk one's "lives, fortunes, and sacred honor" in the fashion of the patriots of the American Revolution in order to be an entrepreneur. There are many varieties and levels of risk-taking. Nevertheless—where there is no risk, there is no entrepreneurship.

OUR SAMPLE OF ENTREPRENEURS AND MANAGERS

Before we talk additionally about the risk-taking characteristics of entrepreneurs, it would be a good idea to discuss the sample of entrepreneurs and managers we examined in the empirical study that supports our conclusions.

With the financial and reputational support of the Kauffman Foundation, we contacted 501 American CEOs and asked them to participate in our study, which relied both on surveys and interviews. CEOs could utilize

Table 3.1 Derivation of the CEO Sample

Number of CEOs contacted	501
Number of CEOs who agreed to participate	303 *(60.5 percent of those contacted)*
Number of CEOs who provided a completed a survey	253 *(50.5 percent of those contacted)*
Number of CEOs who provided a completed and usable survey	234 *(46.7 percent of those contacted)*
Number of founding CEOs in final sample	102 *(43.6 percent of final sample)*
Number of non-founding CEOs in final sample	132 *(56.4 percent of final sample)*

the Internet to complete our survey instrument, if they wished. A very satisfactory 303 (60.5 percent) agreed to participate and a gratifying 234 (46.7 percent) eventually provided us with a usable survey instrument. Of these individuals, 102 were founding CEOs (43.6 percent of the final sample) and 132 (56.4 percent) were non-founding CEOs ("managers"). Table 3.1 summarizes these data.

The participants in the sample ranged from the CEOs of single-employee ventures to the CEOs of *Fortune 500* enterprises. Slightly more than 79 percent were Caucasians and 83 percent were men. While 44 percent had completed an advanced college degree, fully 11 percent had not completed high school. Slightly more than 17 percent were military veterans, and their average age was fifty-four years. Table 3.2 reports these data.

Appendix 1 supplies much more detailed information on both the sample and the survey instrument. It will suffice for us to observe that we utilized a stratified, random sample technique to contact our CEOs and our survey response rate was well above any comparable study. It was not always easy to convince CEOs to provide us with the great volume of personal information we requested and therefore we utilized a variety of persuasive techniques to

Table 3.2 A Brief Summary of the Characteristics of the CEOs in Our Sample

83 percent men, 17 percent women
79 percent Caucasian, 21 percent minority
11 percent did not complete high school
19 percent completed high school
26 percent attended college
44 percent completed college and an advanced college degree
17 percent were military veterans
Average age: 54 years

convince them to trust our promise of anonymity. One CEO frankly told us we were crazy if we thought he would give us the wealth of information about him and his firm that we desired. While this business leader later did complete the survey, his worry was that we had been sent by one of his devious competitors.

CEOs who participated in our study could respond either by sending us their completed survey via the U.S. Mail or by completing the survey and transmitting it to us via the Internet. Almost 70 percent of founding CEOs utilized the Internet to complete and return their survey, while only 52 percent of non-founding CEOs choose that path. As our survey information subsequently will reveal, the founding, entrepreneurial CEOs in our sample were more comfortable utilizing technology in their operations. While one should avoid reading too much into our "how did they return the survey" information, it does not take a leap of logic to infer that founding CEOs in general tend to be more open to change and more receptive to new innovations. Those are among the personality traits associated with entrepreneurship. Use of the Internet (and perhaps the CEO's trust in it) may well serve as a modest proxy for their entrepreneurial traits.

ENTREPRENEURS AS CHANGE AGENTS

The behavioral genetics research we reviewed in the previous chapter strongly supports the notion that some individuals are born with a predilection to involve themselves in situations that bode to change the existing state of affairs. Some individuals thrive on change. As a high-technology CEO we interviewed expressed it, "I literally can't help it. I like to change things and upset the apple cart. I would be no good at all running a conventional outfit in a stable industry."

We posit that entrepreneurs (those who have founded their own firm) are much more likely to be change oriented than CEOs who did not start the firm they are managing. This is the natural order of things. The reason most entrepreneurs founded their own firm is that they wanted to change something—perhaps how products are made, how they are marketed and sold, or how and where they are used. Often they possess a sweeping vision of how that change will occur. Juan Trippe, who founded the Aviation Corporation of America (which later morphed into Pan American Airways), firmly believed that he could profitably fly passengers to worldwide destinations and in the process render many cruise ships obsolete. Trippe was not interested in managing an established industrial giant such as U.S. Steel, for he was driven by an enticing dream about how long-distance travel could be revolutionized.

CONVINCING CEOs TO PARTICIPATE IN OUR SURVEY PROVED TO BE A DAUNTING TASK

We were aware that MacCrimmon and Wehring had obtained only a 14.4 percent response rate in their well-regarded 1984 study, but hoped we could do better. Eventually, we did exceed this standard substantially, though it was a struggle to do so and required numerous telephone calls and much follow-up by us. In due course, 46.7 percent of all CEOs we contacted provided us with a usable survey instrument; this is a commendably high percentage for a study such as this. Nonetheless, even though we presented each prospective participant with an impressive set of endorsements, often by a prominent business official from their trade association or a regional Chamber of Commerce, the CEOs, in general, were very reluctant to complete the survey instrument. Or, once they read and digested our instrument, almost 20 percent of those who agreed to participate nonetheless apparently decided against completing it. Dozens of CEOs told us that they did not want to disclose the information we were asking them to give us, despite our assurances of confidentiality. In contrast to more than 700 college and university presidents who supplied us with similar data for our study that was published as *The Entrepreneurial College President*, some CEOs simply did not trust us. Nor, apparently, would they have trusted any academic researcher.

The Question of Ownership

There is a critical feature of Juan Trippe's story that we must not neglect. Trippe and most entrepreneurs have direct financial motivation to succeed. They own some or all of the stock of the firms they have founded. Their leadership skills, or lack thereof, translate directly to their personal bottom financial lines. If their firm loses money, then they lose money. Their personal fortunes and those of the firm they have founded are joined at the hip.

Contrast the personal financial interest of a founding entrepreneur in her firm with that of a famous non-founding manager, Robert Nardelli, who led Home Depot from 2000–2006. As the national media repeatedly noted, Mr. Nardelli received $245 million in compensation for his services during that time even though the price of Home Depot's stock fell 12 percent. Meanwhile, the share price of its chief competitor, Lowe's, rose 173 percent during the same period.[4] These very different results elicited howls of protest about Mr. Nardelli's compensation because there was an apparent disconnect between Home Depot's value in the marketplace and Nardelli's pay. This led some to query what Nardelli would have been paid had Home Depot's stock price soared? In any event, Nardelli was sacked in 2006 but subsequently emerged a year later as the chairman and CEO of automaker Chrysler Corporation.

Economists label the Nardelli/Home Depot situation a "principal-agent" problem. The underlying question is this—how can stockholders (the principal) get CEOs (their agents) to behave and lead efficiently, and not to slack off and shirk? Literally, how can stockholders convince CEOs to act like entrepreneurs whose next paychecks and even their jobs depend upon their leadership success?

Historically, stockholders and boards have attempted to provide incentives to non-founding CEOs by compensating them with shares of stock, that is, by making them partial owners. Thus, when the firm does well and its stock price rises, then the CEO's wealth rises accordingly. Clearly, such an arrangement does provide some incentive for a CEO to perform well, but will not necessarily prevent a Home Depot scenario from reoccurring.

Further, we should not forget that a firm's stock price may rise due to a generally rising stock market or because of external economic events that have little or nothing to do with CEO competence and performance. Unfortunately, it's also true that crafty CEOs may have the ability to influence the share price of their firm's stock by deciding how and where to report the firm's revenues and profits. The bottom line is that giving CEOs an equity interest in their firms is not a foolproof way to accelerate their performance. Nevertheless, evidence suggests that stock incentives, appropriately framed, positively affect CEO performance.

DOES MANAGERIAL OWNERSHIP MAKE A DIFFERENCE?

A recent study published in the *Journal of Financial Economics* found that 43 percent of the managers of mutual funds own a stake in the funds they manage. These managers earned an 8.7 percent rate of return on the assets they managed in 2005; the rest of the managers (the ones who didn't have a stake in their fund) earned only a 6.2 percent rate of return. Each 0.01 percent increase of fund assets owned by the fund manager improved the fund performance by 0.03 to 0.05 percent (Khorana, Servaes, and Wedge, 2007).

In our survey sample, ninety-three of our 102 founding CEOs owned stock in the firm they founded, whereas only sixty-two of the 132 "managers" (non-founding CEOs) owned stock in the firm they were leading. The critical question here is, did this make a difference? Yes it did, according to our data. The firms led by founding CEOs grew at a rate of 23.5 percent per year and earned a 31.2 percent rate of profit on their invested capital, while the firms led by non-founding managers grew at a rate of 12.4 percent annually and earned a 17.1 percent rate of return on their invested capital.

Of course, these observed differences in growth and profit rates could be due to other factors such as the nature and maturity of the industry in which particular firms compete, the business cycle, and so forth.[5] Many other factors could be responsible for the startling differences in growth rates and profit rates we observed between founding and non-founding CEOs. Therefore, these data are supportive of our argument, but certainly do not prove it.

It seems quite likely that entrepreneurial CEOs and managerial CEOs self-select. Those CEOs that are not entrepreneurially inclined gravitate to more predictable firms and industries, while entrepreneurially inclined individuals grab for the brass ring and found their own firms. Edwin Locke (2000, p. 87) offers brief vignettes of entrepreneurs ("prime movers" in his terminology) ranging from J.P. Morgan and Cornelius Vanderbilt to Steve Jobs and Warren Buffett. Such individuals were not cut out emotionally to become clerks or college professors. The lure of entrepreneurial activities attracted them like iron shavings to a powerful magnet, for it is entrepreneurship that enables them to realize their life's ambitions. Locke describes them thus:

Prime Movers are enormously ambitious. They differ from other people in the scope and intensity of their ambitions, in the fact that they love their work, and in their actions taken to succeed. These ambitions may be expressed in terms of money or in terms of work accomplishments that will earn money, or both.

Locke's glimpses of these individuals support our basic thesis that some individuals are naturally cut out to be entrepreneurs, while others are not.

Measures of CEO Orientation Toward Change

How do the 234 CEOs in our sample describe themselves when the subject of change is broached to them? Table 3.3 reports the responses of our CEOs to statements about their own attitudes with respect to change. Each CEO could issue one of five responses to each of these statements—a "1"

Table 3.3 CEOs, Innovation, and Entrepreneurship

Characteristic	234 Sample CEOs	102 Founding CEOs	132 Non-founding CEOs	Statistical significance attached to difference
Frequently think outside the box	3.63	4.36	3.07	.000
Generate lots of innovative ideas	3.90	4.63	3.34	.000
Enjoy stirring things up	3.75	4.08	3.50	.000
Encourage creative individuals even when they disagree with me	4.40	4.34	4.46	.298
Frequently violate the status quo	3.44	4.21	2.84	.000
Violate the chain of command	3.71	4.42	3.16	.000
Believe in organizational structure	2.10	1.97	2.20	.017

indicates a statement with which they strongly disagreed; a "2" indicates mild disagreement; a "3" indifference; a "4" mild agreement; and a "5" strong agreement.[6] Hence, in the case of the statement, "(I) enjoy stirring things up," all of the CEOs together averaged a 3.75 response, while founding CEOs averaged 4.08 and the non-founding managers a 3.50. Thus, all of the CEOs taken together believe they tend to stir things up, but entrepreneurs are much more likely to believe this. *Prima facie*, this supports the hypothesis that founding entrepreneurs are much more likely to want to be change oriented than the other CEOs.

The final column in Table 3.3 contains an estimate of the statistical significance of the difference between the responses of the two groups of CEOs.[7] Statistical significance here may be interpreted as the response to this question—"If we took another sample of equivalent size of CEOs and each in turn reacted to the same statement about stirring things up, how likely is it that we would reject the result we have just uncovered and instead declare that there really isn't any difference between the two groups?" The 0.000 level of statistical significance tells us that this would occur in less than 1 in every 1,000 new random samples of CEOs that we might choose to take. This level of statistical significance tells us that we can be rather confident in the difference we found between the two groups of CEOs.

A perusal of the data in Table 3.3 also reveals that founding entrepreneurs are much more likely than other CEOs to view themselves as thinking outside the box and as individuals who generate lots of innovative ideas. They also are much more likely than ordinary CEOs (non-founding managers) to see themselves as violating the status quo and also as individuals who violate the chain of command. In addition, they are less likely to believe in organizational structure.

MANAGERS OR LEADERS?

Richard Kovacevich, Chairman and CEO of Wells Fargo Bank, aptly expressed the sentiment of many entrepreneurs when he outlined what he perceived to be the difference between "managers" and "leaders." "Managers rely on systems, leaders rely on people. Managers work on getting things right, leaders work on the right things" (cited in Slatter, Lovett, and Barlow, 2006, p. 9). Transactional CEOs tend to be "managers" in Kovacevich's lexicon, while transformational CEOs tend to be "leaders" who have a propensity to subvert or go around organizational structures and instead deal directly with key people in order to accomplish change.

In this regard, our interviews revealed that entrepreneurs often are frustrated by organizational structures. "I want to get things done," asserted an entrepreneur in a manufacturing industry, "and the bureaucracy in this place gets in my way." He uttered these sentiments despite the fact that he was the person that created, or at least did not stop the development of, that bureaucratic organization!

In this vein, the secretary to Sam Walton (of Wal-Mart fame) spoke with a bit of awe about Mr. Walton: "If he gets something in his mind that needs to be done—regardless of what else might have been planned—the new idea takes priority, and it has to be done now" (Walton and Huey, 1992, p. 116). Mr. Walton was not afraid to reach up or down Wal-Mart's organizational hierarchy in order to get that "something" accomplished.

Note that these results *do not prove* that differences actually exist between entrepreneurs and other CEOs with respect to how they view innovation, disruption, and change. Nevertheless, such evidence does provide considerable support for the notion that entrepreneurs are different. At the very least, both entrepreneurs and non-founding CEOs think they are different. And, it is clear that others perceived them as being different. The general thrust of the evidence is clear. Entrepreneurs welcome change and thrive in periods of disruption when new patterns of behavior are being established. Conventional CEOs, however, often shy away from change and prefer stability. Indeed, some non-founding CEOs may hide behind the organization or utilize a collective bargaining agreement to explain why they cannot initiate changes that might undermine their situation.

The evidence in Table 3.3 strongly suggests that if you enjoy stirring things up, frequently think outside the box, generate lots of innovative ideas, frequently violate the status quo, often violate the chain of command, and do not strongly believe in organizational structures, then you're much more likely to become an entrepreneur. Since behavioral genetics evidence indicates that these characteristics appear to be heritable, this implies that some individuals are born with a predisposition to enjoy stirring things up and disturbing the status quo. Over time, our evidence suggests, a sorting process occurs and such individuals are more likely to move into entrepreneurial leadership positions.

Nor does this sorting process exist only for profit-oriented business leaders. Our analogously based work with more than 700 college presidents indicates that college presidents broadly acknowledged to be successful are distinctly more entrepreneurial than their run-of-the-mill brethren (Fisher and Koch, 2004). It should not surprise the reader to learn that the most successful college presidents are entrepreneurial types who enjoy stirring things up and who are not afraid to take risks. They believe they can change their institution (and the world) for the better. Witness well-known and highly successful college presidents such as Father Theodore Hesburgh at Notre Dame, Steven Trachtenberg at George Washington, and Steven Sample at University of California, Los Angeles (UCLA). These academic leaders were entrepreneurial agents of change.

WHERE DO ENTREPRENEURS COME FROM?

Our sample of CEOs was generated from the following geographic regions of the United States:

Northeast	17.9 percent
Midwest	31.2 percent
South	26.1 percent
West	24.8 percent

Shane (2008) argues that rates of entrepreneurship are not highest in the Silicon Valley, around Route 128 near Boston, or in Austin or Seattle, but rather in the Midwest and more remote locations such as Vermont. He points out that higher rates of unemployment and lower incomes ordinarily are associated with the starting of more new businesses.

Historical evidence suggests these entrepreneurial relationships also exist in most other occupations and professions. Even the military, thought by many to be a "by the book," non-innovative segment of society, sometimes reflects these entrepreneurial imperatives. Highly successful generals

Table 3.4 CEO Risk-Taking and Attitudes Toward Risk

Characteristic	All 234 CEOs	102 Founding CEOs	132 Non-Founding CEOs	Statistical significance attached to difference
Am risk-averse	1.94	1.54	2.25	.000
Believe leaders take risks	4.42	4.43	4.42	.925
Have made decisions that could have cost me my job	3.70	4.57	4.02	.000
Firms should insure themselves against risks	2.44	1.93	2.84	.000
Believe diversification is the primary way to combat risk	3.86	4.15	3.64	.000
Believe in quantitative risk assessment	3.29	3.88	2.84	.000
Use software to help monitor risk	3.20	4.01	2.57	.000
Believe risk assessment is primarily subjective	2.35	1.78	2.80	.000
Risk and return are positively related	3.82	4.28	3.45	.000
Believe I am responsible for compliance with regulatory and financial rules	3.30	4.14	2.56	.000

case of this CEO, he was not attempting to hedge the prices of inputs and products he had to purchase, but was instead actively attempting to make money by predicting the future course of prices of commodities that had little or nothing to do with his business. "It's all my money," he advised us as he moved to his computer screen and entered a "put" on a copper commodity mix even as we talked.[8] It will suffice for us to observe that such individuals are indeed different from the run-of-the-mill CEOs.

Entrepreneurial CEOs told us that they believe in quantitative risk assessment—more so than managerial CEOs. The entrepreneurs also are more likely to utilize computers, spreadsheets, and software to help them make their judgments about risk. By contrast, a *Fortune 500* CEO in our sample told us that he believes risk assessment is primarily a subjective task. "Ultimately, it is my gut feeling, my intuition, that tells me whether I should proceed on a venture," he confided. He warned against becoming "overly scientific" about risk assessment and investment analysis and cautioned against "number crunching." Interestingly, his opinions on these

such as Erwin Rommel and George Patton in World War II, ;
Schwarzkopf in the Middle East in 1990, possessed the willing
conventional thinking and their orders often relied upon the
surprise. They were prolific generators of innovative ideas anc
entertained "outside of the box" people and ideas.

Were such entrepreneurial individuals born to their tasks?
so. Everyday life tends to sort out entrepreneurial individuals,
select roles and occupations where they can exercise their entrej
inclinations. This is true not only for business CEOs, but also for t
exercise the leadership of non-profit institutions (where entrep
activity unfortunately often can be conspicuously absent).

OUR EMPIRICAL EVIDENCE ON CEOs AND RISK-TAKING

Both founding, entrepreneurial CEOs and the other, non-fou
managerial CEOs believe that excellent leaders must take risks. Tl
little difference between them on this score, as Table 3.4 reveals. Intel
CEOs understand, at least intellectually, that quality leadership means
than standing still. However, Table 3.4 also reveals entrepreneurial (
are less risk-averse than regular CEOs by a wide margin. Though they l
that risk-taking is necessary, the non-founding CEOs are more likely t
risk-averse than entrepreneurial CEOs. Further, the entrepreneurial C.
who have founded their own firm are much more likely to report that t
have made decisions that could have cost them their jobs.

One way for risk-averse individuals to deal with perceived risks is
purchase some type of insurance. When asked to react to a stateme
indicating that firms should attempt to insure themselves against risks, tl
non-founding, managerial CEOs were much more likely to concur wit
that sentiment. A non-founding CEO said to us, "I try to be the pruden
man described in the law and undertake due diligence before I do anythin;
important."

Many individuals and stockholders might prefer such a "prudent" CEO.
However, an entrepreneurial CEO aptly characterized the difference between the two groups of CEOs by opining, "You can't buy insurance for
the types of risks I take. I'm not driving a car; I'm investing most of my life
savings. Who is going to insure that?" He went on to express the view of
several other entrepreneurs that CEOs who attempt to insure themselves
against everything end up taking no real risks at all.

One intrepid entrepreneurial CEO we met not only did not attempt
to insure his firm against risks, but even deliberately increased the risk
exposure of his firm and himself by operating in future markets. In the

matters broadly reflected the views of the 132 non-founding CEOs in our sample.

A representative entrepreneurial CEO demurred at this approach. He advised, "You surely can't quantify everything, but you can do your best to lay out the pluses and minuses connected to a deal. You are negligent if you don't try to compute the present value of future revenues and costs." Another entrepreneur forthrightly exclaimed, "It's my money I'm risking, not somebody else's. I'd be a bit loony not to try to figure out what's going on." He also offered, "CEOs who haven't put their own sweat and blood into their own firm might do things differently, and perhaps depend upon someone else to do the analysis for them, but I couldn't live that way."

One of the fundamental principles of investment and portfolio analysis is that risk and return are positively related. That is, holding other influences constant, ordinarily one cannot expect to earn a higher rate of return on an investment without being willing to assume additional risk. This is one of the reasons why the rate of return one expects to realize on a highly secure ten-year U.S. Government bond is lower than the rate of return one expects to realize on a bond given a grade C by Standard and Poor's, or a speculative investment in a mutual fund composed of stocks from the developing countries of Asia.

Managerial, non-founding CEOs, despite being slightly better educated than the entrepreneurial CEOs, were much less likely to believe that higher risk usually accompanies the promise of higher rates of return. Indeed, several managerial CEOs offered the view that there was relatively little risk attached to most of the decisions they made. One emerged with the sense that they viewed their firms as running almost on auto pilot. "We're doing well," observed one such CEO, "and my biggest job is to avoid messing things up. I keep people working together, referee disputes, keep people in a positive mood and thinking about the future, and represent us externally."

The reader may regard as straw men the entrepreneurial CEO we have quoted ("It's my money I'm risking, not somebody else's.") and the non-founding, managerial CEO ("... my biggest job is to avoid messing things up"). However, the tenor of the data in Tables 3.3 and 3.4 indicates these statements are more representative of the differences between entrepreneurial and non-entrepreneurial CEOs than many management gurus previously have hypothesized. The difference between the two groups may not be separated by a chasm, but it is at least a steep gully and it is apparent that they have differing views of the world and risk-taking.

Note that these contrasting views of risk-taking are a direct implication of behavioral genetics research, which tells us that some individuals are endowed with the urge to take risks and institute change, while others are not. It is evident that entrepreneurial ventures tend to attract a different type of person than non-entrepreneurial activities. Simply put, business CEOs are no exception to this general rule.

Some Experimental Evidence

There is one additional, rather telling bit of evidence from our surveys that speaks clearly to the risk-taking differences between entrepreneurial and other CEOs. We confronted each of the 234 CEOs in our sample with several hypothetical choices. The first exercise asked them which of the following two choices they preferred:

A: $1,000 with absolute certainty $(p = 1.00)$

B: $2,050 with a probability of one-half $(p = .5)$ *and* $0 with a probability of one-half $(p = .5)$

Here "p" represents the probability that an event will occur. Thus, choice A means the CEO will receive $1,000 with absolute certainty $(p = 1.00)$, with no risk of default. Choice B, however, would provide the CEO with $2,050 half the time $(p = .5)$, but give him absolutely nothing the other half of the time $(p = .5)$. One can see that choice A always will produce $1,000 without fail, while choice B will *average* a $1,025 payoff ($2,050 × 0.5 + $0 × 0.5 = $1,025). Individuals who are risk-averters will prefer choice A to B because choice A presents no risk of loss and almost the same return. However, depending upon how much risk an individual likes to take, a risk-lover might well opt for choice B.

Our founding CEOs preferred choice B 79 percent of the time, while the non-founding CEOs preferred choice B only 43 percent of the time. This conceptual experiment once again demonstrates a critical difference between the two groups of leaders concerning how they perceive and relate to risky situations.

The choices just presented are relatively simple, and choice B does not even involve any prospect of an actual loss. Let's complicate the picture slightly by introducing the prospect of a financial loss. Consider the following two choice options:

C: $1,000 with absolute certainty $(p = 1.00)$

D: $3,000 with a probability of one-half $(p = .5)$ *and* −$600 with a probability of one-half $(p = .5)$

Choice C is identical to our previous choice A; the CEO who chooses it always receives $1,000 without fail. Choice D, however, is more complex.

Half of the time, Choice D produces a $3,000 *gain,* but the other half of the time, choice D involves a $600 *loss.* The CEOs who opt for choice D will, on average, earn a $1,200 payoff ($3,000 × 0.5 + −$600 × 0.5 = $1,200).

When confronted with choices C and D, our founding CEOs preferred choice D to choice C 71 percent of the time, while our non-founding CEOs preferred D to C only 32 percent of the time. Thus, our founding CEOs preferred D to C more than twice as often as the non-founding CEOs.[9]

Our evidence highlights the reality that individuals often see the same facts differently. A situation that one individual interprets as an attractive opportunity may be seen by another as an unattractive, looming threat. Individual perceptions of risk differ and this is an important reason why some people become entrepreneurs, others managers, and still others workers. Significant aspects of these differences are hardwired into their respective individual genes.

Can education and experience overcome these instinctive differences in perceptions and preference? Perhaps, but the evidence we have just presented reveals that even an MBA degree may be insufficient to overcome the innate and overwhelming tendency of some CEOs to be risk-averse and fearful of change.

The CEOs Assess External Risks

Our CEOs face the rigors of managing the risks facing their companies and dealing with a wide variety of competitive pressures on a daily basis. In addition to confronting the CEOs with hypothetical choices, we also asked them to tell us how they assessed various aspects of the risks they face in their environments. In the words of one CEO we interviewed, "You want to know what worries us the most, don't you?" Table 3.5 provides some insights in that regard.

The CEOs rank changes in their customer base as their most important concern, followed by the changing activities of their competitors and fluctuating prices for the things they must purchase. Variations in stock prices and interest rates, the dangers of a deteriorating society and natural disasters (including terrorism) trailed these top three worries by a considerable amount. Statistically significant differences between founders and non-founders emerged only with respect to changing competition, a deteriorating society, and natural disasters. Founding CEOs worry less about their competition and more about the deterioration of society and natural disasters. These views may be consistent with their higher levels of political conservatism and also could account for the increased time and energy they spend in their communities compared to non-founders.

Table 3.5 CEOs Evaluate Their Environment and the Risks They Face (Here's how I rank the importance of the risks that my organization faces in the following areas (1st, 2nd, 3rd, 4th, 5th, and 6th):

Risk	All CEOs	Mean rank Founding CEOs	Non-founding CEOs	Statistical significance
Changing competition	2.69	2.49	2.84	.041
Changing customers	1.85	1.87	1.91	.345
Changing interest rates and bond prices	4.38	4.46	4.32	.490
Deteriorating society	4.22	4.60	3.93	.004
Natural disasters	4.18	4.56	3.89	.006
Changing prices of inputs	3.28	3.26	3.30	.868

DOES IT MAKE A DIFFERENCE WHAT YOU STUDY?

Given the differences we have observed between founding CEOs and other CEOs, it is natural to inquire after the sources of these differences. Are they innate or are they acquired? While this question is, as we already have seen, exceedingly complex and does not easily lend itself to testing that would provide a definitive answer, we already have taken the position that the weight of evidence suggests many of these differences are innate.

However, if one believes that managerial skills, risk-taking attitudes, and entrepreneurship can easily be taught and learned, then this encourages one to search for the times and places where this teaching and learning occur. Precisely, when and where does this learning occur? Needless to say, a profusion of teaching–learning opportunities exist, beginning in the home when children are very small and extending throughout an individual's lifetime.

An obvious location where teaching and learning occur is colleges and universities. However, almost 30 percent of our CEOs did not earn a baccalaureate degree and slightly more than ten percent did not graduate from high school. Nonetheless, for those CEOs who did attend college, does it make any difference what course of study they pursued?

Approximately one-third of our CEOs earned an MBA degree or near equivalent. It is a virtual certainty these individuals have taken courses in disciplines such as accounting, economics, and statistics that traditionally have been foundation stones in MBA programs. In recent decades, disciplines such as computer science and psychology have elbowed their way onto this list of essentials. Still, does this make any difference?

We put the question to all of our CEOs (including those that did not attend college)—Have you taken a minimum of one course in each of

Table 3.6 Does the Academic Background of a CEO Affect CEO Performance?

	All CEOs	Founding CEOs	Non-founding CEOs	Statistical significance
Have taken accounting course	59%	64%	55%	.259c
Have taken computer science course	62%	67%	59%	.447c
Have taken economics course	63%	71%	57%	.098c
Have taken psychology course	50%	59%	43%	.055c
Have taken statistics course	65%	73%	57%	.052c

the following five academic disciplines (accounting, computer science, economics, psychology, and statistics)? Table 3.6 records their responses. Sixty-five percent of the CEOs indicated they had taken some type of course in statistics (however defined) while 63 percent reported they had taken a course in economics, and 62 percent in computer science. Fifty-nine percent of the CEOs reported they had taken a course in accounting, and 50 percent had taken a course in psychology.

Interestingly, the founding CEOs have taken each of these five courses more often than the non-founding CEOs, but statistically significant differences exist only for economics, psychology, and statistics. In each of these cases, the founders took these courses more often than the non-founders. If one subscribes to the view that managerial skills, risk-taking, and entrepreneurial essentials can be learned, then one is tempted to attribute some of the differences between the two groups of CEOs on these characteristics to their collegiate experiences. However, one cannot attribute cause and effect here because a degree of self-selection appears to exist with respect to such courses. To wit, if I'm thinking entrepreneurially, then I'm probably more likely to take an economics course rather than an art history course. Hence, it is easy to argue that an individual's appearance in an economics class (or any other course seemingly related to entrepreneurial activity such as accounting or finance) is a product of their genes and personality traits. That is, they are naturally inclined toward such rather than such courses making them entrepreneurs. Clearly, this is an area that would benefit from more research. At this point, we must be satisfied with noting that behavioral genetics research supports the hypothesis that a variety of entrepreneurially oriented personality traits are heritable. In fact, the burden of proof is upon business schools and related educational efforts to demonstrate that they actually produce additional entrepreneurs rather than simply hone the existing personality traits and skills of their students.

CAN AN EXAMPLE SUM IT UP?

One of our entrepreneurial CEOs founded his own financial firm about one decade ago. This firm specializes in hedging, a process by which traders attempt to profit from their perceptions that the prices of certain stocks and other financial instruments either are overpriced or underpriced. For example, a firm that engages in hedging might decide that shares of General Motors stock are underpriced and consequently undertake a set of actions designed to profit if that perception turns out to be reality. It is fair to say that many hedgers, and the CEO we visited in particular, live in an environment characterized by immense financial risks, and they operate in this world on a daily basis. Success often depends upon their taking advantage of momentary price differentials in financial assets and making a trade a millisecond faster than a competitor. This CEO proudly told us that he has gained and lost more than $100 million in a single day. He observed, "The fact that I'm still here means I've been right more times than I've been wrong."

Some of the CEOs to whom we talked would find dealing with such high levels of risk absolutely disabling if they had to do so on a consistent basis. As one of them put it to us, "I couldn't get out of the bed in the morning if I thought I might lose my house and everything I have in a couple of hours." Nevertheless, when we visited with the hedge-oriented CEO, he looked out over what he referred to as his war room, which at that very moment was jammed with gesticulating, occasionally profane traders and their assistants huddled in front of computer terminals, and exclaimed to us, "@#$%, isn't this great!"

Some of the CEOs to whom we talked would find dealing with such high levels of risk disabling if they had to do so on a consistent basis. As one of them put it to us, "I couldn't get out of the bed in the morning if I thought I might lose my house and everything I have in a couple of hours." Nevertheless, when we visited with the hedge-oriented CEO, he looked out over what he referred to as his war room, which at that very moment was jammed with gesticulating, occasionally profane traders and their assistants huddled in front of computer terminals, and exclaimed to us, "Isn't this great!"

His exultation, side by side with the other CEOs' timidity, ultimately is the story of this book.

RANDOMNESS AND OUR SAMPLE: A TECHNICAL NOTE

Even though we have deliberately avoided most of the statistical and mathematical questions related to our work in order to make it accessible to more individuals, before we move on to other topics, we should spend a few moments talking about the nature of the sample that has generated the results we have begun to report. If discussions such as these turn you off, then turn a few pages and go on to the next chapter!

Despite the various challenges noted above, we did end up with a sizable sample ($N = 234$) and an admirable response rate. Indeed, given the quantity and depth of data that we requested from the CEOs, this is the largest CEO sample ever assembled on these topics. Some survey-based studies have developed larger samples (for example, MacCrimmon and Wehring, 1986), but no study of our size has assembled the wealth of information about CEOs, their risk-taking activities, and their personalities that we have. Further, our relatively high response rate diminishes, but certainly does not eliminate, the effects of non-response bias.

Our initial approach to the 501 CEOs we contacted was based upon stratified random sampling techniques designed to generate a sample that would simultaneously reflect the national pool of CEOs in terms of demographics, type of firm, and geography, and enable us to compare founding CEOs with other, non-founding CEOs. Eventually, 157 (67.7 percent) of the responses of the 234 CEOs in the sample were generated via this route. Not surprisingly, however, we found that the larger the firm and the more ostensibly important the CEO was, the less likely he was to respond positively to our survey request. Therefore, we had to depart from classic randomness to request specific CEOs (sometimes individuals we knew) to complete the survey. As noted, this was particularly necessary for the CEOs of large firms. But, it was also necessary for us to depart from strict randomness in the case of minority CEOs, CEOs in manufacturing industries, and CEOs located in New England. For a variety of reasons, these individuals did not respond at high rates. Thus, we engaged in "quota sampling" (as this practice is known in statistical literature) in order to ensure that a sufficient number of cases existed in our major CEO categories of interest.

What this means is that our data are not based upon a strict random sample drawn from the larger population of all CEOs. "Semi-random" or "substantially random" are perhaps the most accurate ways to describe our sample. Our personal requests to selected CEOs ("Please complete this survey") who were not a part of the stratified random sampling process represent a departure from strict randomness, but were specifically designed to replicate the overall population of CEOs and entrepreneurs and to produce a final sample in which at least 40 percent of the participants would be founding CEOs (this latter constraint required "differential sampling," as the practice is known in statistical literature).

The statistical challenges associated with nonrandom sampling are well known (Alexander et al., 1986). Measures have been developed to determine the extent to which nonrandomness results in critical bias that alters statistical results (Copas and Li, 1997). Such measures typically assume, however, that one has the ability to compare random results with nonrandom results and note the differences. Of course, we cannot do that and very few researchers in similar situations can do so either, because if they were able to do so, then they would in most cases have from the start chosen a random sampling technique.

This does not necessarily suggest that our sample is not representative of the overall population of CEOs. In fact, we believe our final sample of 234 CEOs is more representative of the actual population of CEOs than the sub-sample of 157 CEOs that responded to our stratified random sampling. By way of illustration, no *Fortune 500* CEOs responded to our stratified random sampling, but we were able to convince five *Fortune 500* CEOs to participate in the study when they were contacted personally. Similarly, we were able to double the percent of minority CEOs participating in the study by means of personal approaches to them. Hence, the 234 CEOs in our final sample are, we believe, more representative of the true universe of CEOs than samples that would be produced by random sampling techniques.

The reality is that many studies based upon putatively random sampling are nonrandom after all because of nonresponse biases (for example, those CEOs and entrepreneurs who have failed and gone out of business are unlikely to become members of the sample), or because of a variant of Berkson's fallacy whereby those who agree to participate in a study have different characteristics than the underlying population. As Copas and Li (1997) observe, "Randomization becomes a model for the data rather than a factual statement of how the data were obtained" (p. 55).

The nonresponse phenomenon is particularly vexing. In many survey studies, only 10 to 20 percent of those who are sampled actually respond. As previously noted, MacCrimmon and Wehring's capable 1984 survey drew a 14.4 percent response rate. By comparison, our response rate is much higher, and therefore it is plausible that our sample is at least as representative of the underlying population of CEOs as that of MacCrimmon and Wehring. Still, heroic assumptions often are required to conclude that no patterns of importance exist among either nonresponders or responders. We prefer to be up-front about the quota sampling that we have undertaken in order to fill out critical portions of our sample instead of accepting a much lower response rate and assuming away any nonresponse bias.

The test of the pudding is in the eating, and we believe that our final sample is an accurate representation of the CEOs who lead American firms today. The tables we present below, we believe, support this contention. Still, our departure from randomness means that several of the statistical techniques we utilize must be evaluated with departures from classic randomness in mind. A degree of prudence always is called for in survey-based empirical work and our situation is no exception. To the extent that our sample is nonrandom, statistical tests that assume randomness may be unreliable. Hence, we will exercise analytical caution. But, nearly every statistical caveat that applies to our study realistically also applies to purportedly random studies.

In any case, one never "proves" a meaningful, falsifiable theory. Instead, one gains more or less confidence in it as an explanation of the world. In this spirit, our work supplies useful information that enables us to improve our understanding of CEOs, their risk-taking, and their personalities. We do not claim to be writing a new version of the Ten Commandments. Our work, therefore, does not represent the final words on the issues we examine.

Chapter 4

Entrepreneurial Management and Leadership Style

Leadership is the ability to decide what is to be done and then get others to do it.

—Dwight D. Eisenhower, 34th President of the United States

When the eagles are silent, the parrots begin to jabber.

—Winston Churchill, British Prime Minister

Whenever you see a successful business, someone once made a courageous decision.

—Peter Drucker, American business author and advisor

If Ralph Waldo Emerson (1841) was correct when he opined that "An institution is the lengthened shadow of one man," then the firms and organizations we observe in the real world ultimately will reflect the style and quality of the leadership and decision making of their CEOs. Indeed, with respect to founding, entrepreneurial CEOs, it is difficult to argue otherwise. They founded their company, have lived and died with it, and except in unusual cases that company now necessarily reflects their management preferences, habits, and biases.

Entrepreneurial CEOs and managerial CEOs do manage their firms differently. However, as Table 4.1 discloses, both groups of CEOs believe they make decisions easily and further that they confine themselves to what they perceive to be the big decisions. Both groups of CEOs say they place a high value on consensus. There is little difference between the self-perceptions of the two kinds of CEOs on these scores.

However, entrepreneurial CEOs realize they are somewhat less likely to delegate responsibility to subordinates than non-founding CEOs. Indeed, our interviews with entrepreneurial CEOs and their employees suggest that many entrepreneurial CEOs may in their surveys have exaggerated the extent to which they actually delegate responsibility to others. They perhaps responded how they would like to be viewed rather than how they actually operate. A vice president of a medium-sized firm providing office services whispered to us with a grin, "She [referring to her boss] keeps her fingers on everything. Not much of anything happens around here without her knowledge or approval."

In common parlance, more than a few entrepreneurs are micromanagers and they admit as much when talking privately. Sometimes this stems from the fact that when they founded their firm, they had to do everything in order to survive. A representative entrepreneurial CEO told us with some pride that he could, and still did, function as a jack-of-all-trades. "I did it all—I did our books, constructed our first data base, and even did some plumbing when the toilets wouldn't work." We found only one "hired," non-founding CEO who claimed to have performed analogous tasks.

FREDDY HEINEKEN, THE FOUNDER OF THE DUTCH BREWING GIANT

Freddy Heineken once asserted that "I consider a bad bottle of Heineken to be a personal insult to me." Heineken's passion and devotion to the quality of his product are acknowledged to be an important reason behind the international success of the beer (Van Munching, 1997). Edwin Land, the inventor of the Polaroid camera, was so invested in his firm and research that he would telephone his colleagues at 5:00 a.m. (Evans, 2004). Micromanagement, or least strong attention to details, is a two-edged sword not without its benefits.

Nor do some entrepreneurial CEOs ever lose the tendency to get involved at any and all levels of their firms. Raymond Damadian, one of the inventors of magnetic resonance imaging (MRI), who became famous for taking out a full-page, sour grapes advertisement in the *New York Times* when he did not receive a perhaps deserved Nobel Prize, was a brilliant man. However, Evans (2004) describes him an as obsessive, relentless individual, and his coworkers found him often unable either to delegate authority or to accept others' achievements. William Shockley, the inventor of the semiconductor, was a micromanager par excellence whose management skills were noticeably primitive. Shockley constantly intruded on the work of his colleagues, demeaned his employees, and was what today we would call a "boss from hell." Like many impetuous, strong-willed, and impatient entrepreneurs, he had trouble retaining employees and colleagues. Shockley is not the first genius entrepreneur to discover that not everyone shares his commitment, drive, and enthusiasm.

MICROMANAGERS ARE COMMON AMONG ENTREPRENEURS

The authors once evaluated a highly effective college president who had served with great distinction in that position for several decades at the same institution. This vigorous, successful individual personally approved nearly every expenditure his institution made and once even amended a requisition to reduce the number of doughnuts that could be served at a meeting. Micromanagement, then, is hardly confined to the for-profit sector. However, it appears to be a more common phenomenon common among entrepreneurial and long-tenured CEOs.

THE VALUE OF COMMITTEE MEETINGS

One telling tip-off relating to the issue of managerial delegation of responsibilities is the aversion entrepreneurial CEOs have to committee meetings. As Table 4.1 illustrates, they tend to regard committee meetings as a waste of time and prefer individual, one-on-one meetings. An entrepreneurial CEO involved in real estate somewhat ironically confided to us, "I really do want to hear the opinions of others, but I just don't want to wait very long to hear them."

Another entrepreneurial CEO had framed in his office a large picture of several stationary hippopotami situated in a circle. Every one of the huge animals had open, gaping mouths resplendent with gigantic teeth and appeared to be having an animated conversation. The picture was accompanied by an admonitory sentence: "In the final analysis, lots more is said than ever is done." This was his way of saying that many committee meetings wasted valuable time and that, in his words, "The mark of an excellent CEO is his ability to ensure that meetings actually contribute some value." The picture also sent a message to those who entered his office—actions speak louder than words.

Table 4.1 Entrepreneurial Decision Making

Characteristic	All sample CEOs	Founding CEOs	Non-founding CEOs	Statistical significance attached to difference
Make decisions easily	4.06	4.09	4.04	.870
Confine myself to the big decisions and leave smaller decisions to others	2.74	2.75	2.73	.908
Place a high value on consensus	3.37	3.38	3.36	.826
Delegate extensive responsibility	3.68	3.59	3.75	.219
Count committee meetings as mistakes	3.70	3.91	3.55	.002
Believe in the value of one-on-one meetings	2.91	3.04	2.82	.111

In fact, many CEOs, entrepreneurial and otherwise, often know the course of action they want to take before they schedule a meeting and therefore undertake consultation primarily as a last and final check on their wisdom. However, some CEOs are so skillful at leading their meetings that their colleagues are left guessing what the CEO's agenda actually was. The danger in such situations, of course, is that fearful subordinates will shy away from offering complicating facts or contrary views to the CEO because they "don't want to get in the way of a streamroller" (the words of the chief financial officer of a corporation founded and still led by a highly successful entrepreneur). As Warren Buffett, the "Oracle of Omaha," has pointed out, in these circumstances, usually "his internal staff and his outside advisors will come up with whatever projections are needed to justify his stance. Only in fairy tales are emperors told that they are naked." Employees usually come to understand that "the boss" (as one small firm entrepreneur was described to us by his employees) wants them to "be a member of the team" and that he prefers consensus, if not enthusiasm, behind the plan (his plan) and a minimum of nay-saying. If there is nay-saying to be done, it is advisable to do so in private with the CEO.

Entrepreneurial CEOs, as we have seen, have a predisposition toward action. They are confident, energetic, even exuberant individuals. They want to do things, and not tomorrow, but today, or even yesterday. "When it's time to act, I act," was the unmistakable injunction to us from a founding CEO, who added, "People who have to rely on organizational charts to run their business aren't going to be successful."

If anything, entrepreneurs tend to be overconfident and frequently over-estimate the extent of their own skills and knowledge as well as their overall chances of success. A 1988 study of almost 3,000 entrepreneurs found that fully one-third believed that chances of their success were 100 percent and 81 percent believed their chances of success were 70 percent or better (Cooper, Woo, and Dunkelberg, 1988). In fact, however, a substantial majority of newly founded firms fail. Shane (2008) reports that only 29 percent of all firms founded in the United States in 1992 were still alive and functioning ten years later.

We do not mean to suggest that all entrepreneurial CEOs are over-confident and have unrealistic expectations. Many behave differently. For example, in one scientific firm we visited, the CEO regularly sponsored small meetings that essentially functioned in the fashion of an advanced academic seminar. Ideas were "thrust out on the table" (the opinion of a member of the firm's scientific advisory board) and then "everybody would take their shots." This process exposed shallow thinking and placed a spot-light on less-than-obvious risks, the board member reported. The end result was that unreal expectations and conspicuous, unmerited overconfidence usually were deflated.

Nevertheless, such rational, probing analyses usually are the exception rather than the rule among entrepreneurs, who frequently act out of passion and a persistent, not easily discouraged belief in their own intelligence and acumen. Both our data and interviews lead to the conclusion that entrepreneurial CEOs ultimately rely relatively less upon the opinions and views of others than non-founding, managerial CEOs. The two groups of CEOs both may *listen* to their colleagues, employees, and board members in equal proportion, but entrepreneurial CEOs eventually are more likely to discard discordant views and move ahead. They are less inclined to take votes on important issues and usually make no bones about this.

To use leadership terminology, entrepreneurial CEOs usually are not transactional in their behavior. Typically, they do not spend a great deal of time thinking how they can please or persuade their colleagues, thereby hoping to gain their support. Instead, they are passionate, transformational leaders on a mission who fully intend to change the existing state of affairs and therefore have a greater tendency to disregard discouraging views or evidence. Without question, they sometimes can be impulsive and precip-itate in their actions and rash in drawing conclusions. They *know* what they want and are focused on what they need to do. The contrary views of individuals they regard as members of the establishment they wish to over-throw often only spur them to disregard warnings or pessimistic forecasts. Because they *know* what is right, a few contrary straws in the wind are quite unlikely to convince them otherwise.

If other observers perceive that the odds against them are steep and tell them so, they often simply interpret this as a challenge. "Even my wife told me I was crazy," noted one entrepreneur, who ruefully described to us how he failed in three entrepreneurial efforts before achieving conspicuous success. One entrepreneurial failure told us he took hope from the experience of Howard Schultz, the founder of Starbucks, who was spurned by more than 200 investors and financial institutions before obtaining funding (a story that does not appear to be apocryphal; see Schultz and Yang, 1999). It's notable that the entrepreneur who cited the Starbucks example eventually did obtain the funding he needed to pursue his own dream, but failed to make it successful.

STAYING IN TOUCH VERSUS SOCIAL DISTANCE

Entrepreneurial CEOs tend not to relish committee meetings, but they do want to be in close touch with what's going on in their firm. As Table 4.2 reveals, they walk the floors of their company more often than other CEOs. Indeed, when we gave additional attention to these data, we found that those entrepreneurial CEOs who lead very small firms or who tend to micromanage easily are especially likely to appear on the production floor, talk with employees, to have lunch with supervisors, or to visit a branch of the firm.

By contrast, the non-founding CEOs were less likely to intrude into other areas of their firms even though they were more likely to hold the view that they should develop close personal relationships with their employees. "I want my people to know that I care about them," observed a non-founding CEO. Given their reduced tendency actually to walk the floors of their firms and interact directly with employees, non-founding CEOs tend to rely more heavily upon written communications and Web site information to "tell their story" (a description supplied by a *Fortune 500* CEO).

Entrepreneurial CEOs, on the other hand, tended to stress being visible and available to their employees, though not developing intimacy. "I eat lunch in the company cafeteria several days a week and go and sit down with the janitors, or the computer programmers, or whoever is there," reported an entrepreneurial merchandising CEO. "But," he added, "I don't take those relationships outside of work hours."

Like the most successful college presidents, founding CEOs instinctively seem to prefer to maintain some degree of social distance from their employees. The founding CEOs as a group also report that they believe they have developed a measure of mystique in their relationships with their employees. "They certainly know me," said an entrepreneurial CEO, "but they don't know all that much about me and my private life."

Table 4.2 Entrepreneurs and Their Employees

Characteristic	234 Sample CEOs	102 Founding CEOs	132 Non-founding CEOs	Statistical significance attached to difference
Frequently walk the floor of my company	2.82	2.99	2.68	.004
Believe in close personal relationships with my employees	2.85	2.57	3.07	.000
Maintain a measure of personal mystique	3.44	4.11	3.11	.000
Believe respect from those I lead is crucial	4.55	4.73	4.41	.001
Like people who are different	3.83	4.49	3.32	.000
Attempt to develop a diverse work force	3.78	4.34	3.34	.000
Believe in merit-based compensation	3.96	4.45	3.63	0.000

Slatter, Lovett, and Barlow (2006) hit it on the head when they quoted an executive who cannily observed, "I don't need friends at work . . . respect will do very nicely, thank you" (p. 6). It's difficult to retain charisma and even authority when one has become fast friends with employees. Close friends get to know each other's weaknesses and foibles, and this can lead to a loss of influence if they occupy different rungs on the organizational ladder and one reports to the other. Further, it can be quite awkward for a leader to evaluate close friends, sometimes because close friendships between a leader and a follower lead to the spread of rumors, especially if the leader and friends are perceived to have the potential for a sexual relationship. Charges of favoritism by the boss and sycophantic behavior on the part of employees are endemic when a leader and follower become strong friends. Witness the travails of Mary Cunningham, who went to work at Bendix Corporation as the executive assistant to CEO William Agee in the early 1980s and subsequently was quickly promoted to a vice president's position. This generated prolific office rumors, considerable resentment, and anonymous letters of complaint to the Bendix Board of Directors. The complaints alleged unfair treatment, unmerited promotions and compensation, and an affair between Cunningham and Agee. Both parties vigorously denied the allegations, but the damage had been done to both of their reputations. Two years after Cunningham departed from Bendix for a vice presidency at Seagram's, they married.

All things considered, wise executives maintain a degree of social distance between themselves and their employees. Entrepreneurial CEOs seem instinctively to understand this principle, though as one founding CEO put it to us, "I'm going at such a high rate of speed that I don't really have time to develop close relationships with anyone." Another entrepreneur, who has founded a half-dozen firms, noted that close relationships were never a problem for him because he always was selling out and moving on before strong personal friendships could develop.

A highly successful high-technology entrepreneurial CEO proudly confessed to us his perception that some of his employees "regard me somewhat like a rock star." He averred that everybody knew him and could shake his hand, but he was always on stage, a somewhat glamorous figure slightly removed from them.

It is well worth observing that these entrepreneurial managerial perceptions and habits are related to leadership success. Both leadership theory and empirical evidence reveal that social distance is a source of leadership power (see Fisher and Koch, 1996, for a summary). Leaders who become excessively familiar with those they lead gradually lose their ability to lead and inspire. Their inspirational mystique and power dissipate because they have become just one of the crowd. It's difficult to be charismatic with individuals who know one's innermost thoughts and dirty laundry.

This does not suggest that leaders should avoid being visible and involved. Those CEOs who walk the floors of their plants, eat lunch with their employees, and value one-on-one meetings understand this, but they also wisely intuit that they "can't be one of the boys" (the words of an entrepreneurial CEO) if they want to retain employee respect and their ability to lead, inspire, and motivate.

It is apparent that all of the CEOs in our sample understand that the respect of their employees is crucial, but this is especially true for the founding CEOs. These entrepreneurial individuals, more than 10 percent of whom did not graduate from high school, instinctively grasp that a degree of social distance is an important way to cultivate and maintain that respect.

PEOPLE OF DIFFERENT VIEWS, DIVERSE WORK FORCES

Entrepreneurial CEOs are more apt to report that they like to mix and meet people who are different and to develop a diverse work force. In a moment of candor, and buttressed by anonymity, a non-founding, managerial CEO opined, "In college, I read the book, *The Organization Man* about conformity in American large business firms and corporations [Whyte, 1956].

There's a certain amount of that here. People who don't immediately fit the mold are slowly bent into shape."

On several occasions, non-founding, managerial CEOs told us their job was to "manage the corporation" and "not to halt or destroy our progress." Stability was a word that came to their lips much more often than for entrepreneurial CEOs, and free-thinking individuals might damage that stability "and throw us off track." In this, they reflected the famous admonition of Chester Barnard in his oft-reprinted *The Functions of the Executive* (1938), which can be summarized as follows:

The responsibility of the executive is (1) to create and maintain a sense of purpose and moral code for the organization; (2) to establish systems of formal and informal communication; and (3) to ensure the willingness of people to cooperate.

These are laudable aims, but noticeably absent is any mention of entrepreneurial leadership, transforming the organization, or dealing with change. Still, this description of leadership responsibilities is not far from the mark insofar as many of our non-founding CEOs are concerned. Compared to entrepreneurial CEOs, we found fewer non-founding CEOs to be men and women of passion who had strong agendas for change. As a consequence, by their own reports in our surveys, they do not see much to gain from associating with individuals who have challenging views, or who might shake the stability of their organization.

Interestingly, even though non-founding CEOs indicated lower support in our surveys for developing a diverse work force, our interviews with them did not reveal a lack of *verbal* support for affirmative action. Instead, these CEOs substantially regarded affirmative action as someone else's business. "I don't hire very many people at all," observed a non-founding CEO, "and so it's really up to the vice presidents and division heads to do those things."

This view is revealing in that it discloses this non-founding CEO's ultimate lack of personal attachment to the activities and performance of his corporation, which ranks among the *Fortune 500*. However, on the other side of the fence, entrepreneurial CEOs displayed a much greater personal identification with their firms and, in the words of one CEO from a firm that ranks among *Fortune's 1000*, "I'll have to admit that I live and die with nearly everything we do. This is my reputation and legacy we're talking about."

As one can see in Table 4.2, entrepreneurial CEOs expressed a much greater interest in having a diverse work force than did non-entrepreneurial CEOs. Whether or not this was for them a matter of moral conviction cannot be discerned, though one stated this was spurred by his religious beliefs "to do good" and to hire minority employees. We can say, however, that our interviews disclosed utilitarian motives for developing a diverse work force. One entrepreneur confessed, "I need the support of the city and the state and they look closely at such things." Another offered the view that employees with diverse backgrounds tended to be more innovative and "I like the fact that they see things through different lenses."

Entrepreneurs frequently relish the opportunity to meet nonestablishment individuals and other innovators, if they believe such individuals can help them realize their entrepreneurial visions. One entrepreneur expressed it this way: "I like to hear different political points of view and I've traveled to places like Tierra del Fuego and Kazakstan. I patronize what some people might regard as avant garde art studios. I also spend quite a bit of time talking with professors and other inventors about what they're doing. But, I'll admit that I am not interested in someone coming into my firm and sowing discord. So, I like smart, independent guys who nevertheless can play within our rules, which I think are rather loose compared to many firms I know."

It is important to understand that the differences we have drawn between entrepreneurial CEOs and managerial CEOs are matters of degree. The two groups of leaders are different on a variety of measures, but this does not signify that all CEOs in these groups think and act in concert. In many cases, there is at least as much variability inside one of the CEO groups as there is between the two CEO groups.

MERIT-BASED COMPENSATION

Merit-based compensation systems are anathema in many non-profit organizations. Teachers unions usually must be bludgeoned to accept merit pay, and most teachers' contracts do not include pay clearly based upon performance. Hence, it should be no surprise that most public school systems are largely bereft of entrepreneurship.

By contrast, both groups of CEOs in our sample believe in merit- and performance-based compensation and this is especially true for the founding CEOs. Whether or not they subscribe to the predictions of economic theory, entrepreneurial CEOs nearly always implement merit pay in their firms. "I reward performance; it's that simple," exclaimed a CEO who queried, "How could I do it otherwise, if I want to earn a profit?" Another entrepreneur, this one leading a firm with about 100 employees, forthrightly exclaimed, "I reward and I punish by means of the raises I give. But my financial rewards and punishments are more than that. I'm also handing out recognition and giving people a pat on the back, or a warning. Every raise or promotion that I give sends a signal."

Whatever the views of the CEOs in our sample, research suggests that effective leaders often strike an enviable balance between use of carrots and sticks (which merit-based compensation represents) and inspirational, charismatic leadership. Successful leaders correctly conclude that compulsion and penalties can lose much of their impact if used repeatedly, even in many authoritarian societies (again, see Fisher and Koch, 1996, for a summary). Our founding CEOs appear to understand this instinctively because they regard the respect of their employees as absolutely crucial to their success even while they attempt to use merit-based compensation judiciously to elicit desired behavior. Incentives do make a difference, as the demise of the former Soviet Union and the rise of the People's Republic of China clearly demonstrate. Even so, skillful leaders mix inspiration, team-oriented values, and incentives to generate superior overall performance.

MISCELLANEOUS MANAGERIAL CHARACTERISTICS

Many entrepreneurs are loquacious individuals, sometimes to their detriment. Their extroversion leads them to be interested in a wide variety of people and topics and they often offer their viewpoints to their employees, friends, and the media. Table 4.3 divulges that entrepreneurial CEOs often speak spontaneously, much more often than our other CEOs. One of our non-founding CEOs confirmed this when he told us that he usually speaks in what he termed "set-piece situations," that is, situations where he or someone else has prepared his remarks ahead of time and where post-remarks questions can be anticipated or controlled. Like many other non-founding CEOs, he worries that extemporaneous remarks may cause more problems than they solve, particularly where labor relations are concerned.

On occasion, vocal CEOs, and especially entrepreneurs, get into trouble with their remarks. Mark Cuban, a serial entrepreneur whose achievements include broadcast.com, which he sold for $5.9 billion in Yahoo stock, provides an extreme, but fascinating, example. Currently the owner of the successful and profitable Dallas Maverick National Basketball Association (NBA) team, Cuban has been fined more than $1.6 million for more than a dozen statements that the NBA has found objectionable. Dirk Nowitzki, the Mavericks' superstar player from Germany, pungently observed

He's got to learn how to control himself as well as the players do. We can't lose our temper all the time on the court or off the court, and I think he's got to learn that, too. He's got to improve in that area and not yell at the officials the whole game. I don't think that helps us. . . . He sits right there by our bench. I think it's a bit

Table 4.3 Filling In the Gaps

Characteristic	234 Sample CEOs	102 Founding CEOs	132 Non-founding CEOs	Statistical significance attached to difference
Seldom speak spontaneously	3.12	2.46	3.64	.000
Involve spouse in company business	3.02	2.62	3.34	.000
Believe management skills can be taught	2.12	1.93	2.39	.000

much. But we all told him this before. It's nothing new. The game starts, and he's already yelling at them. So he needs to know how to control himself a little.[1]

The Mark Cuban scenario holds interest for us beyond the fact that it demonstrates the difficulties that CEOs can encounter if they do not carefully monitor their utterances. However, Cuban's activities also suggest that on occasion micromanagement can backfire. If employees believe they are under especially intense scrutiny, some of them may not perform at their best.

The most effective CEOs, empirical evidence and our interviews reveal, maintain what we would label "a knowledgeable presence" within their firm. They are visible within the confines of their firm and they often communicate with their employees, formally and informally. Typically, they do not micromanage. They delegate appropriate responsibilities, but demand accountability. Their employees emerge with the feeling that they have a degree of independence in their activities, and that their individual judgment is valued, but also perceive that their work is being appropriately monitored and evaluated.

To be sure, we encountered several entrepreneurial CEOs who violated nearly all of the prescriptions recited in the previous paragraph, yet were leading expanding and profitable firms. Strong external demand for a firm's product often can overcome most of its managers' missteps. Still, in the confessional words of a dot-com entrepreneur, "We probably would be doing even better if I were a better manager."

Most of our CEOs (88 percent) were married. We found that among our entrepreneurial CEOs, especially in the early days of their firms, it was commonplace for their firms to rely heavily upon CEOs' families to "fill in the cracks and get things done." This practice was especially true for spouses, some 80 percent of whom were women. "My wife was and still is my bookkeeper," allowed the entrepreneurial CEO of a 20-employee firm, "and my son used to be my major salesman." However, as entrepreneurial firms grow, their CEOs typically become more likely to part ways with family members.

Even so, how much do CEOs involve their spouses (usually a wife) in activities related to their business, whether work, entertaining, or whatever? Surprisingly, our 132 non-founding CEOs indicated that they were more likely than our 102 founding CEOs to utilize their spouses for some purpose within their firms. We regard this as an unexpected finding in that it is clear that many small entrepreneurial ventures rely heavily upon family members immediately after they are founded.

Nevertheless, several entrepreneurial CEOs told us that their wives were themselves entrepreneurs who valued their own activities and independence. "My wife doesn't want to be tied down by my company activities," advised an entrepreneurial CEO. "She has her own small business and lots of other gigs." If this is broadly true, then it inspires another hypothesis that we must confess we did not test, namely, that assortive mating is common among CEOs. That is, it may be the case that entrepreneurial men and women tend to marry other entrepreneurial men and women. This is a plausible proposition. After all, evidence indicates that marital pairs in general do tend to sort themselves on the basis of characteristics such as education, religion, and race. Perhaps they do so as well on the basis of their passion for change and entrepreneurial activities.

Whatever be a CEO's managerial philosophy and tendencies, can management skills be taught? That is, can we teach individuals to be superior managers? This is a critical question, and the answer turns substantially upon how we define management. If management skills are confined to knowledge of accounting principles, minimum wage law requirements, patent licenses, social security obligations, and the like, then the answer appears to be a definite yes, these things can be taught. However, if management includes entrepreneurial skills, then we already have offered the view based upon research that it is quite difficult to teach entrepreneurial skills. This is not withstanding the fact that many universities attempt to teach entrepreneurship to their students. What is most difficult to impart, however, are the essentials of an entrepreneurial personality.

Yahoo!Finance's Web site expressed its suspension of belief in the entrepreneurial merits of MBA programs, which is as follows: "For a while now, it's been clear that the true entrepreneurial geniuses don't need degrees. The most effective way to learn about entrepreneurship is to practice in real life. You don't need an M.B.A. for that" (Trunk, 2007).

What do our CEOs believe on this issue? Non-founding CEOs are more likely to believe that managerial skills can be taught, though even they evince substantial doubt that this task can be accomplished. A founding CEO spoke for others when he commented that "We pay the tuition and fees of employees who take college courses leading to a degree or a certification we need. In most cases, however, it is the process of completing the degree that tells us more about the employee than the actual knowledge they acquire. If they can earn a decent degree, probably they can write reasonably well and think logically. Those are the most important things for us, not whether they have completed Management 101 at a university. We can teach them the detailed things we want them to know on the job."

CAN ENTREPRENEURSHIP BE TAUGHT?

Professor Donald Kuratko, who enthusiastically teaches entrepreneurship at Indiana University, feels so strongly that entrepreneurism can be taught that he exclaimed, "... the question of whether entrepreneurship can be taught is obsolete" (2005, p. 577). It is plausible that technical and informational aspects of entrepreneurship can be taught, for example, how to write a business plan, read balance sheets, etc. Yet, as the evidence we have surveyed strongly suggests, it is very difficult to teach someone to be a risk-taker, or to prefer situations involving ambiguity and change. These personality traits associated with entrepreneurial behavior appear to have strong heritability. Either you have them, or you don't.

A discerning founding CEO remarked that, "It's really difficult to determine if someone has an appetite for tackling the unusual, working with difficult people, or dealing with threats. Grades don't tell you much about these things." He went on to say that his company needed more adventuresome people, "not really river boat gamblers," he argued, "but people who understand that everything is not nailed down, people who can see new openings, and who can develop new ventures." He did not use the word entrepreneur, but the absence of entrepreneurial individuals in his firm was the object of his concern. Apparently he did not believe conventional college course work could teach such things.

Many of our CEOs, then, utilize collegiate education and degrees as sorting mechanisms that help them and their firms identify which job applicants are intelligent, can stick to a job, and complete work on time. But they seldom use education and degrees as a way to determine who is entrepreneurial. A founding CEO who leads a large restaurant chain told us, "I use college degrees as a gate keeper. If I see that an applicant has completed an M.B.A. degree at a good school, then this gives me confidence that this person is more likely to have some of the qualities that we need

Table 4.4 Entrepreneurial Loyalty

Characteristic	234 Sample CEOs	102 Founding CEOs	132 Non-founding CEOs	Statistical significance attached to difference
Place firm before myself	3.81	4.48	3.30	.000
Would move to a better position at another firm	2.63	1.82	2.55	.000

in our operation. The classroom knowledge may be useful, too, but I'm looking for smart people who are going to show up for work on time, understand directions and complete their projects. Degrees help me figure that out."

Warren Bennis, a highly published scholar on the subject of leadership, has asserted, "Leaders must encourage their organizations to dance to forms of music yet to be heard."[2] Both groups of our CEOs are disinclined to believe that one can teach employees to "dance to forms of music yet to be heard," though most appear to believe they can provide opportunities for those so inclined to do so. Can non-entrepreneurially inclined CEOs create such an atmosphere? The answer to this question is not clear. However, our data and behavioral genetics research discourage one from believing so. Their concerns with stability and their own personalities do not augur well for their ability to supercharge an entrepreneurial atmosphere.

LOYALTY TO THE FIRM

Many individuals view non-founding CEOs as hired guns, individuals whom established firms employ to manage those firms. Because they are "hired help," as one non-founding CEO described them, and may not own very much, if any, of the firm they manage, it is plausible that their commitment to their firm—their current employer—may be less than that of founding, entrepreneurial CEOs, most of whom own some or all of their firm.

Table 4.4 addresses this hypothesis. When asked, do you place your firm before yourself, a dramatically larger proportion of entrepreneurial CEOs indicated that they believe they do so. "I love this place and I put in a huge number of unpaid hours of work that only I know about. I don't think I would do so if the sign outside didn't have my name on it," responded an entrepreneurial CEO.

For many entrepreneurs, their firm is their life's work and they regard it almost as they do their own children. An entrepreneurial CEO who founded a trucking firm that has grown from four employees to almost 500 in the space of a decade disclosed that he recently had received and declined a buyout offer from a larger trucking firm. Had he accepted this lucrative offer (he would have netted $25 million, he told us), he would have become a divisional vice president at the larger acquiring firm. This CEO echoed Napoleon Bonaparte, who, having led his armies to victory, declared "I can no longer obey; I have tasted command, and I cannot give it up."[3]

The trucking CEO had tasted the thrill of entrepreneurial leadership and was not about to bequeath his pride and joy to someone else. But, contrast him to our group of non-founding CEOs. Table 4.4 reveals they are much more likely to be willing to move to a "better" position at another firm. Of course, what is better is always in the eye of the beholder. Nevertheless, the data in Table 4.4 indicate that entrepreneurial CEOs are more loyal to their firm and much more willing to sacrifice their own time, resources, and welfare in order to make their firm prosper. Surely this finding cannot come as a surprise; it does, however, once again underline another of the many significant differences between founding entrepreneurial CEOs and the rest.

Chapter 5

Entrepreneurial Habits
and Preferences

The lucky fool [is] a person who benefited from a disproportionate share of luck but attributes his success to some other, generally very precise, reason.

— Nassim N. Taleb in *Fooled By Randomness: The Hidden Role of Chance in the Markets and in Life*, 2001

One machine can do the work of fifty ordinary men. No machine can do the work of one extraordinary man.

—Elbert Hubbard, 1923

The family is a haven in a heartless world.

—Attributed to Christopher Lasch

Once upon a time, there was a successful male CEO who agreed to accompany his wife to her high school reunion. During the social hour, they met a downtrodden fellow who used to date his wife in the days of yore. Since then, this poor guy had not been very successful and now was an hourly employee at a fast-food operation. This prompted the confident, "full of himself" CEO to remark to his wife, "You know, if you hadn't married me, you'd probably be married today to that loser." His quick-witted wife retorted, "Well, if you hadn't married me, that's exactly what you'd be doing today!"

The lesson is that CEOs and their performance do not exist in a vacuum. All CEOs have some kind of a family relationship, even if they are unmarried or are an only child. Most, however, have, or have had, a wife or husband and children who have helped or hindered their progress.

In addition, CEOs have social connections, and perhaps political beliefs, and a religious preference. In this chapter, we probe those relationships and ask, for example, whether the wife in our story is correct. Does a spouse affect a CEO's behavior and performance? Are entrepreneurs more, or less, likely to be married and to have children? Are entrepreneurs more inclined to political and religious activity than other CEOs, or is it the reverse? These are among the interesting questions we will address, and for the most part, they have never been explored in a large sample study of entrepreneurs.

FAMILY CHARACTERISTICS OF ENTREPRENEURS

Do entrepreneurs have "Ozzie and Harriet" families and, if so, do they differ in that regard from non-entrepreneurial CEOs? Table 5.1 helps answer this question. Relative to our non-founding CEOs, our founding, entrepreneurial CEOs are more likely to be currently married and less likely to ever have been divorced. They also have larger families (more children) and themselves grew up in a larger family (more brothers and sisters).

These data suggest several intriguing, though eminently arguable hypotheses. First, the values and activities of entrepreneurs might cause them to prefer traditional family relationships—a husband or wife and children. Perhaps the stability conferred by families is attractive to individuals whose business lives are very different and involve substantial risk-taking and an arduous struggle for survival. Families may function as refuges for entrepreneurs.

But we must issue a note of caution. Entrepreneurs are more likely to get married, stay married, and have larger families. However, it does not logically follow that these characteristics make it more likely that someone will become an entrepreneur. Getting married and having a large family may not result in someone becoming more entrepreneurial. The most we can say is that these characteristics are outcomes, not causes, of entrepreneurial activity.

Nevertheless, some do argue that there is something about large families that makes individuals who grow up in them more likely to become entrepreneurs. This notion possesses surface plausibility because several entrepreneurs told us they grew up in large families where competition among siblings was commonplace. Even so, we would remind our readers

Table 5.1 CEO Marital and Family Characteristics

Characteristic	All sample CEOs	Founding CEOs	Non-founding CEOs	Statistical significance attached to difference
Number of marriages	1.76	1.32	2.09	.004
Number of children	2.18	2.38	2.02	.012
Number of siblings	2.10	2.50	1.79	.000
Father's highest level of education (years)	13.4	13.1	13.6	.707
Mother's highest level of education (years)	12.3	12.0	12.5	.715

that science does not encourage the notion that family size has much to do with entrepreneurship. The studies of twins we reviewed earlier in this book suggest that family environment is relatively unimportant in determining adult personality traits such as extraversion and a preference for novelty seeking. The twin studies and behavioral genetics do not support the supposition that the number of siblings has much, if anything, to do with adult risk-taking.

We noted earlier that 11 percent of our CEOs did not graduate from high school. Table 5.1 now tells us that the typical CEO's parents were not highly educated either. Overall, the fathers of our CEOs completed 13.4 year of education (that is, one plus year of college) and the mothers of our CEOs completed 12.3 years of education (slightly more than high school). In both cases, the parents of non-founding CEOs are somewhat better educated than the parents of the entrepreneurial CEOs, but those differences are not large.

These data lend emphasis to our discussion of the impact of family environment on entrepreneurship. Though difficult for some individuals to accept, the message of the twin studies and behavioral genetics research is that it is not an entrepreneur's educational level that is crucial to her entrepreneurship, or even the level of education of that entrepreneur's parents. Instead, the single most important factor (though not the only factor) in determining whether an individual becomes an entrepreneur is whether she has certain genes that are conducive to entrepreneurship. It is here that parents come to the fore. Entrepreneurial parents are more likely to pass on entrepreneurial genes to their children than non-entrepreneurial parents. Education may not be irrelevant, but it does not have a substantial impact on the personality traits that are critical to entrepreneurial activity. Several additional years of education are unlikely to make an individual or her parents more extraverted and novelty seeking.

CEOs AND TECHNOLOGY

Fifteen years ago, a Yahoo was an uncultured, boorish jerk. Amazon was the longest river in the world. A Web? It was for spiders. E-mail? Only a few professors and scientists even knew what it was. Now, in the twenty-first century, because of the Internet, these words have acquired new meanings and we pepper our conversations with talk of "dot.coms" and "dot.cons," "logging on," "e-commerce," "surfing the Web," "clicking on icons," and "B2B" sales. Nobody lifts an eyebrow when we say we are going to "Google" someone to find out more about them.

The relevant point is that technology, especially information technology, is an everyday part of the lives of all but the most isolated. In 1950, a CEO might require only minimal technology to complete his duties (a telephone, a mimeograph, and an adding machine). Things have changed. Nearly any CEO, even one who leads a very small firm, can rely upon relatively low-cost telephone service with no-charge long-distance calls, an answering machine, and caller ID; a personal computer that is more powerful than a typical corporate mainframe computer only twenty years ago; a high-speed Internet connection that provides access to boundless information, personalized industry news, and e-mail; and a printer that also serves as a copy machine and scanner. All of these capabilities can be purchased for an approximate $1,500 original investment and a $100 monthly fee. A CEO who is so minded can add a cell telephone for another $50 per month.

Hence, a smorgasbord of technological delights is available to a CEO today. The question is whether or not CEOs actually use such things. Or, do they (in the words of one CEO), "let the others fool around with all of those gadgets, while I use pen, paper, and my typewriter."

As Table 5.2 conveys, an overwhelming majority of CEOs utilize the technologies we have just mentioned. Most carry cell phones, frequently use computers, frequently use the Internet, and require the major executives reporting to them to carry a cell phone or pager so they can be easily contacted. For example, 70 percent of non-founding CEOs and 89 percent of founding entrepreneurial CEOs carry a cell phone.

It's apparent, however, that the entrepreneurs utilize these technologies more heavily than the regular, non-entrepreneurial CEOs. We presaged this result when we noted earlier that our founding entrepreneurial CEOs were much more likely to complete and transmit via the Internet their surveys for this study. It seems clear that the usual founding CEO is more comfortable with technology than the typical non-founding CEO even though many of the founding CEOs operate in prosaic industries that do not appear to be roiled by great change. Thus, one of the founding CEOs in our sample opened a combination beauty salon and barber shop. This is not a line of

Table 5.2 CEOs and Their Use of Technology

Characteristic	All sample CEOs	Founding CEOs	Non-founding CEOs	Statistical significance attached to difference
Carry cell phone	.79	.89	.70	.000
Use computer frequently	.76	.81	.73	.123
Use Internet frequently	.64	.74	.57	.008
Require major execs who report to me to carry cell phone or pager	.72	.77	.68	.117

work that has been turned upside down in recent years as a result of new inventions and innovations. Nevertheless, this entrepreneur told us that she was proud of "having the latest technology" to keep track of her customers and bill them. She proudly showed us how it operated. That said, her hair cuts and perms were, as she confessed, "the same old thing" updated only for recent style changes. Arguably, however, it was her willingness to try something new and her propensity to be willing to take a risk that led her first to open her shop and second to adopt and pay for what she referred to as "gadgets." Vignettes such as these certainly do not prove that founding entrepreneurs are different from other CEOs, but they supply meat for the bones of our basic hypotheses.

"I couldn't get along without my cell phone and Blackberry," exclaimed an entrepreneurial CEO. Another CEO commented that he carried three different cell phones, each dedicated to a different task or public. Thus, he used one cell phone for non-business and family matters. "When a particular phone rings, I already know something about the call and even whether I want to take that call."

Based upon our conversations with CEOs and some of the individuals who report to them, we can predict with some confidence that nearly all of the percentages recorded in Table 5.2 will rise above 90 within a few years. Younger employees and those who will fill CEO slots in the future already use these technologies as a matter of course and think nothing of it. There will always be a distinctive CEO or two who will decide not to carry a cell phone so that she cannot be contacted. And, there always be those who find face-to-face communication more effective than e-mail, especially in small businesses. Even so, the trend toward greater reliance upon technology is unambiguous.

One of the heaviest users of personal technology among the CEOs is an engineer who leads a dot.com. He issued a strong caveat. "When you become dependent upon technology, you are up the proverbial creek when it fails to operate. If the Internet goes down, or someone hacks into your computer system, you're in big trouble." (Actually, the CEO used much more colorful language than "in big trouble" here.) Another CEO, less technologically savvy, lamented a weeklong shutdown of his firm's computer system after an uninvited intruder stole virtually all the information the firm had accumulated about its employees—addresses, ages, Social Security numbers, and even some credit card numbers. This required his firm to invest a large sum of money in computer and data security, a task they had heretofore taken too lightly.

CEO BELIEFS AND PRACTICES

CEOs and Religion

As Gartner (2005) has pointed out, portions of the United States were settled by individuals who could easily be termed "religious entrepreneurs." The Puritans, for example, were "in the zealous pursuit of God" (p. 38) and were venture capitalists who perhaps were risking their lives more so than their fortunes in order to establish a new religious order. Since then, however, American society has become more secular and during the twentieth century both church attendance and public expressions of religion declined. Even so, today Americans choose to attend some kind of religious service much more often than many other individuals in the world, especially western Europeans. How is this religious activity connected, if at all, to entrepreneurial tendencies today?

We asked our CEOs whether they attend some sort of religious service two or more times per month. A majority indicated they do so, with entrepreneurial CEOs leading the way. Our CEOs as a group appear, from their reports, to be more religious than the American population as a whole and entrepreneurs especially so.

An entrepreneurial CEO who displayed indicators of his Christian faith in his office declared, only half in jest, "I'd better have God on my side with the kinds of risks I take." Another CEO noted for his risk-taking took pains to tell us that his risk-taking (which he referred to as "gambles") applied to his financial life and not to his spiritual life. Perhaps "born again," he regaled us with a version of the Biblical parable of the talents and told us that God expected each of us to make the most of our talents and opportunities. Thus, he would be derelict in the eyes of God if he did not do his best to improve the world with his entrepreneurial ventures. He argued that "Jesus had an entrepreneurial streak."

The view of religiously oriented entrepreneurs that their daily nonreligious work represents God's calling is nothing new. Gartner (2005) argues that Christopher Columbus was a "messianic entrepreneur" (p. 21) who believed he was the instrument of God. He notes a "sense of moral imperative" (p. 22) among many entrepreneurs whose personalities tend toward unbridled enthusiasm, if not mania.

A cynical, non-founding CEO in our sample who attends church only on occasion suggested to us that his occasional Sunday forays were similar to his attending a Rotary meeting. "I grip and grin before and after services" (shake hands and make conversation), he reported, and he saw occasional church attendance as being good for his business.

Whatever the motivations of CEOs for their religious activities, their reports indicate they are more active in that regard than most Americans. Whereas 73 percent of founding CEOs and 61 percent of non-founding CEOs report they attend a religious service at least twice a month, only 40 percent of all American adults indicate they regularly attend a religious service. This number declines to 10 percent in Europe.[1]

Note once again the direction of causation. Entrepreneurs are more religious; perhaps this is connected with their greater devotion to marriage and the family. We cannot go so far as to say, however, that their religious activity fosters entrepreneurship, though there are researchers (Audretsch, Boente, and Tamvada, 2007) that make the case that certain religions (Christianity and Islam) stimulate entrepreneurs, while others (Hinduism) retard them.

CEOs and Politics

We profess an initial degree of surprise with respect to our survey findings concerning our CEOs and political matters. We were not surprised to find that our entrepreneurs, taken as a group, are politically moderate, even slightly tilting to the liberal end of the political spectrum (by their own estimations). We did not expect, however, to learn that our entrepreneurs were politically more conservative than our non-founding CEOs.

The popular caricature of entrepreneurs is that they are free-spirited odd balls with unconventional habits and tastes. They disdain, even revile the status quo, according to this view. Hence, they are anything but conservatives. Our findings suggest this partial sketch of entrepreneurs is distorted. To be sure, some entrepreneurs are manic and perhaps even a bit weird. Most, however, are not. The typical entrepreneur is a "get up early in the morning, help make breakfast, kiss the wife (husband), and go to work" type of person who also is a soccer dad or mom.

In the popular mind, the term "entrepreneur" often conjures up Silicon Valley inventors who wolf down pizza in their offices at midnight and throw

Frisbees to each other when they want to take a break. The intimation is that such individuals often break with convention and hence are likely to be political liberals, if they bother to vote at all. While our data and interviews clearly reveal that entrepreneurs are different from other CEOs and individuals, the critical differences relate to their willingness to take risks and forge change rather than to their politics, religion, or family lives. Most entrepreneurs are middle of the roaders, politically speaking and that approach also appears to permeate the non-business segments of their lives.

A perusal of entrepreneurial Web sites such as entrepreneur.com and inc.com reveals a dearth of political items. Only when a "really big issue comes up" (for example, relating to patent law, intellectual property, or capital gains tax rates) do entrepreneurs begin to buzz politically. Otherwise, they tend to push politics in the corners of their lives. As the founder and owner of a neighborhood grocery store told us, "I just don't have time for all of that. Anyway, my two cents isn't going to make much difference." Accurate or not, this point of view reflects the feelings of many entrepreneurs (and CEOs in general).

Most entrepreneurs agree with Acs and Szerb (2007), who concluded that governments find it very difficult to influence entrepreneurial activity in the short run. The *Economist* magazine put it this way: "The best thing that governments can do to encourage innovation is to get out of the way" (*Economist*, October 11, 2007). However, there is little argument that in the long run, a well-educated population and institutions such as the rule of law have an impact on entrepreneurial activity. Governments do have an impact upon such things. All one need do is to observe the chaotic conditions that obtain in many sub-Saharan African nations to understand that institutional and environmental factors (including the level of corruption) have a profound influence upon the overall level of entrepreneurial activity in a country. But, these social institutions are enabling conditions and are not very useful in explaining the individual differences in entrepreneurial activity we observe in specific countries.

Like Samuel Gompers, the seminal American labor leader who a century ago advised labor unions to reward their political supporters and punish their political enemies, yet not endorse one political party, most entrepreneurs exhibit remarkable agility in adjusting their support for political parties and particular candidates. As a rule, they are political independents who will climb aboard any political train that will help get them to their destinations. The entrepreneurial CEO of a mid-sized equipment firm said it best: "I contribute to both parties and I make demands of both. I'm interested in results, not ideology. They've got it wrong if they think I'm a true believer."

Table 5.3 CEO Beliefs and Habits

Characteristic	All sample CEOs	Founding CEOs	Non-founding CEOs	Statistical significance attached to difference
Attend religious services twice per month or more	.66	.73	.61	.073
Am politically conservative	2.28	2.41	2.18	.161
Get involved in politics	2.56	1.97	2.92	.000
Dress well	2.96	2.46	3.34	.000
Attempt to avoid the media	3.12	3.18	3.04	.404

Nearly all of the CEOs, entrepreneurs being no exception, articulated an appreciation for the role of government and the need for government "to do things" for them. Even so, several entrepreneurial CEOs expressed some variant of the statement, "most people can make it on their own in America if they really want to." If Andrew Carnegie could start as a penniless, eleven-year-old immigrant bobbin boy and become a multimillionaire, they reasoned, why can't others if they are similarly motivated?

Among the things that many CEOs desired (especially entrepreneurs) was to get governments to "get off our backs" and "reduce their regulations." Non-founding CEOs in publicly traded companies were more likely to complain about the requirements of the Sarbanes-Oxley Act upon their accounting and reporting. A non-founding CEO told us he now understood that he could go to jail if he signed documents that turned out to be misleading or false.

Even though a number of the CEOs held strong opinions about what government should or should not do, as a group they not very likely to get actively involved in politics. Nevertheless, of the two groups of CEOs, non-founding CEOs were much more likely to become involved politically.

Entrepreneurs, then, are a bit more conservative politically than other CEOs. We cannot, however, conclude that political conservatism causes entrepreneurship. Indeed, the relationship could be the reverse—entrepreneurship stimulates political conservatism. The uncertainty here over cause and effect is endemic any time one considers statistical correlations between two variables. The fact that two variables are highly correlated (that is, they tend to move together in the same direction) does not mean one of the variables causes the other. Firemen and house fires are highly correlated; fireman nearly always are present when houses burn. That does not imply, however, that firemen caused or started the house fires.

CEOs and Their Dress

Despite public fascination with the "coolness" of individuals who choose to "dress down" and a society-wide trend toward informality, previous research suggests that successful leaders tend to dress well—at least as well as acknowledged and respected members of the regional hierarchy and leadership (once again, see Fisher and Koch, 1996, for a summary). However, almost needless to say, what constitutes appropriate dress and formality varies from region to region and changes with the venue. Nevertheless, one aspect of leadership is *looking* like a leader.

Andrè Maurois (1940) understood this when he argued that the most important quality of a leader is to be acknowledged as such. It is not for nothing that Supreme Court justices don robes when they hear cases. Their dress, ceremony, position in the room, and comportment deftly signal their authority and leadership. By the same token, dress that is inappropriate to an occasion does nothing positive for a CEO and more likely does harm if he or she does not *look* like a leader.

Our founding CEOs may or may not understand this, but they are considerably less likely than non-founding CEOs to believe they "dress well." In fact, our interviews with entrepreneurial CEOs revealed that many of them "dress down" (perhaps a euphemism). We encountered more than a few founding CEOs sporting sweatshirts and sneakers, plus several men who proudly told us they did not own a suit. This invites the hypothesis that since many of the founding CEOs own their company, they are able to dress as they wish and thumb their noses at the rules that non-founding CEOs may feel constrained to follow. On the other hand, what we may have uncovered here is a simple reflection of the declining importance of formal dress within American society, at least for those who believe they have a choice.

The relevant question is this: does dressing down by CEOs harm their firms in any way? Are casual or even slovenly CEOs less likely to be taken seriously, or to receive a badly needed bank loan, or to be able to convince a customer to purchase their products? We don't know; however, we can say that available empirical evidence with respect to the success of college presidents encourages the view that dress makes a difference (Fisher and Koch, 1996). A college president who has a food stain on his tie is, from the evidence, less likely to convince a potential multimillion donor of the virtues of his request.

One entrepreneurial CEO told us that his dress was "completely irrelevant" both to his performance and that of his firm. He asserted that "I think I gain an advantage when I show up with my dirty, chemical-stained lab jacket on. That tells them that I am a hands-on guy who knows what's going on." He may be correct. What is beyond dispute, however, is that entrepreneurial CEOs perceive what they wear to be less important than other CEOs. Entrepreneurial status may well have an influence on how some individuals dress. The reverse is not true; one's dress does not make an entrepreneur.

CEOs and the Media

Because most firms newly founded by entrepreneurs are small, their CEOs (who may be their firm's only employee) have little need to worry about dealing with representatives of the media. However, even these individuals sometimes confront members of the press who are looking for a story, investigating a crime, or simply want to attempt to demonstrate as one television station puts it, "We're on your side."

As firms grow, however, things change and their CEOs must become more aware of the media. Newspaper stories and television coverage sometimes can make or break a firm. One CEO told us that a timely human interest story about his restaurant that contained lots of additional information had almost doubled his sales. Even so, the typical CEO, founder or otherwise, exhibited a palpable wariness of the media and cited horror stories about media coverage of safety violations, employment practices, and the like as evidence of the destructive potential of the media.

At the highest levels, celebrity CEOs such as Bill Gates of Microsoft, Michael Eisner of Disney, Terry Semel of Yahoo, and Meg Whitman of eBay frequently occupy the media spotlight in the United States. The fall of highly visible CEOs such as Kenneth Lay of Enron, Bernie Ebbers of WorldCom, and Martha Stewart of Martha Stewart Living Omnimedia suggests that extensive visibility, if not notoriety, can lead to problems. Our CEOs, especially those who founded their own firms, appear to be somewhat media shy. On the five-point Likert scale, the CEOs average only 3.12 (very close to the "undecided" response) in response to a query about whether they avoid the media wherever possible. They appear to be rather cautious with respect to the media, understanding that the media can confer fame and free advertising, or catalog problems and failures, real and imagined.

CEOs that must worry about meeting their next payroll are likely to be less inclined to attempt to charm the media. Many CEOs would not excel at working the media even if they tried. Hence, many CEOs "regard those guys [the media] with suspicion" (the comment of a veteran CEO of a large firm), especially when they have little experience in dealing with rambunctious, probing reporters. The data do not reveal significant differences between founding and non-founding CEOs on this score.

The extent to which CEOs speak in public, and how they do so, is not unrelated to how they handl the media. We also asked our CEOs if they agreed with the statement that they seldom speak spontaneously. The founding CEOs in our sample tended to disagree with this statement, as did our successful college presidents in our previous study. That is, they have a much greater tendency to speak spontaneously than the other CEOs. This is, however, a risky strategy that can backfire unless the CEO is both articulate and appropriately cautious. Nearly every media concentration boasts at least one reporter who fashions himself the next Mike Wallace and has learned how to ambush CEOs and elected officials with unexpected questions at unexpected locations. Further, when the CEO leads a publicly traded company, his freedom of speech is constrained and there are certain things he cannot say about his company, its stock, and the like. (In addition, there are other constraints such as not being able to buy and sell stock except during certain designated time periods. This particularly disturbed one founding CEO who muttered, "My God, it's my company. Why can't I buy my own stock?")

Several years ago, we found that many successful college presidents are extremely proficient in using the media to further their institutions' purposes. As a consequence, they actively seek opportunities to tell their institutions' stories and not coincidently pump up their own reputations. But, this practice reflects both a distinctive culture of openness in colleges that also involves notions of shared authority and governance, and much personal observation and practice. Many, perhaps most, CEOs of profit-oriented firms do not operate in such a world and therefore must exhibit care when they decide to cozy up to the media.

Taking a broader view, the empirical evidence on the appropriate speaking habits of leaders and CEOs is mixed. Should one speak only when in a predictable forum and "prepared," or should one seek opportunities to demonstrate breadth and intelligence by speaking in unstructured situations? We know of both CEOs and college presidents who are very skilled at verbal repartee and even spend time on radio talk shows where the danger of being ambushed with difficult, embarrassing, and unfair questions is significant. Founding CEOs may be more prone than other CEOs to do the same because they believe so fervently in what they are doing and relish opportunities to regale audiences with their entrepreneurial stories. Related to this, the hypomanic nature of many founding CEOs also means they have supreme confidence in their own abilities and hence do not shrink from media contacts. Unfortunately, they sometimes bite into poison fruit and later regret what they have said, or find they must issue corrections. It takes skill and experience to deal effectively with the media.

The advent of widespread use of e-mail has added yet another way in which a CEO can utter unwise words that will come back to haunt him. One-time Salomon Smith Barney superstar stock analyst Jack Grubman sent embarrassing e-mails that when made public demonstrated that he had upgraded the rating on a major stock in return for having his child admitted to an elite pre-school in Manhattan.

Those CEOs who regard e-mails as private communications are destined for grief. Like ill-chosen utterances, offensive e-mails not only may anger, they also may be used as evidence in legal proceedings. A wise CEO will not speak or e-mail any statement that cannot bear subsequent public scrutiny. This applies especially to personal, jocular, and romantic messages. What seems funny or romantic at the moment may later appear to be ignorant or immoral. On the basis of our interviews, we believe that founding CEOs are particularly vulnerable to such problems because they regard their company as their property and hence concluded (incorrectly) that their e-mails will never be discoverable.

ARE ENTREPRENEURS FINANCIAL BEHAVIORISTS?

Entrepreneurs, as we have seen, tend to be passionate, enthusiastic, exuberant individuals. Jamison (2004), another Johns Hopkins psychiatrist, notes "Enthusiasm is intoxicating; it goes to the head" (p. 132). She also opines that unbounded enthusiasm can be "dangerous on occasion" (p. 132). The dangers are several. First, some entrepreneurs can be extreme in their behavior. Their emotional highs and exuberance are very high indeed and their emotional lows are deep and dark and test themselves, their families, and their colleagues. Many entrepreneurs experience breathtaking peaks and valleys in their behavior. Gartner (2005), whose definition of entrepreneurship is much more expansive than simply for-profit businesspeople, describes occasions where historical figures such as Martin Luther, Christopher Columbus, Alexander Hamilton, and Andrew Carnegie displayed such up-and-down behavior.

A second danger is closely related. The often messianic character of entrepreneurs causes them to underestimate potential problems associated with their work, as well as to overestimate potential gains and profits. They become the modern equivalent of Voltaire's Dr. Pangloss (1759), who was constantly of the mind that conditions could not be better. Gartner (2005) argues that Christopher Columbus portrayed this overoptimistic condition. "...he greatly underestimated the size of the earth and overestimated the size of Asia's eastward expansion. Both of these

Table 5.4 The Behavioral Finance Hypotheses

Characteristic	All sample CEOs	Founding CEOs	Non-founding CEOs	Statistical significance attached to difference
Regard losses as more important than gains	3.29	3.42	3.18	.117
Tend to be overoptimistic	3.41	3.52	3.27	.071
Tend to overemphasize my own impact	3.39	3.49	.32	.253
Accept losses gracefully	2.88	2.61	3.09	.005
Tend to overemphasize first impressions	3.26	3.45	3.03	.005
Tend to overemphasize personal contacts	2.85	2.93	2.80	.294
Tend to overemphasize small risks	3.62	3.66	3.59	.607

miscalculations conveniently made his proposed journey seem much more achievable than it was" (pp. 24–25).

Related to this, behavioral finance theorists and researchers argue that many individuals are subject to similar cognitive biases that influence their perceptions and interpretations of data and events. Among the biases that entrepreneurs exhibit, according to Simon, Houghton, and Aquino (2000) are overconfidence, an inflated tendency to assume they always can control their own fates, and a tendency to reach conclusions based upon samples that are too small.

We confronted our CEOs with a succession of statements that informally test several of the major postulates and findings of behavioral finance. Table 5.4 records the results. In general, the responses of the founding, entrepreneurial CEOs indicate they are more likely than the other CEOs to exhibit the distortions in perception outlined by behavioral finance supporters. This is consistent with the predictions of behavioral genetics as well as with our interviews.

Kahneman and Tversky (1979) were among the first to explore the implications of behavioral finance. Kahneman was awarded the Nobel Prize in Economics in 2002 for his career efforts in this and related fields even though he had never taken a collegiate course in economics. One of their explorations relates to the asymmetric way most individuals perceive gains and losses. Losses of a given magnitude typically affect decision makers more than gains of the same absolute magnitude. Thus, a $10,000 gain is not perceived to have the same absolute impact as a $10,000 loss. In general, losses have a bigger impact on individual behavior than gains of the same absolute size.

What about our CEOs? Do they recognize this sort of behavior in themselves? Table 5.4 indicates they do not believe they exhibit such behavior. Ironically, the general disbelief by the CEOs that they are *not* susceptible to the perceptual distortion of regarding losses as more important than gains provides support for an important point made by Kahneman and Tversky. Decision makers don't think they are susceptible, but in reality they are. Perhaps the founding CEOs are a bit more honest on this issue than the non-founding CEOs, for our non-entrepreneurs were more likely to agree that they are influenced especially much by losses.

Neither group of CEOs perceives that they tend to be overoptimistic, even though this is a well-documented characteristic in the general population as well as for entrepreneurs. Consider the confident observation of billionaire resort timeshare developer David Siegel, who it has been said, "enjoys life on the edge" (Kroll, 2007, p. 96): "Unfortunately, the people who work for me can't see what I see. I am like a bull who sees red" (p. 98). Siegel admits, earlier in his career, to having been so confident in his judgment that he wrote checks to purchase land even though he didn't have sufficient funds in his account to cover the checks. He then went hat in hand to a series of banks to obtain a loan to cover the checks. By any standard, this is hearty optimism.

The rather pallid response by our CEOs to the notion that they are overconfident embellishes the mentality that stimulated Robert Shiller's best-selling book, *Irrational Exuberance* (2001), which was a play on Federal Reserve Board Chairman Alan Greenspan's oft-cited warning about the danger of inflated asset prices. The CEOs' denials of overoptimism are consistent with the prediction of behavioral finance, namely, that many individuals tend to be overoptimistic but don't realize it. In fact, the evidence is that most individuals exhibit a consistent optimistic bias, particularly with respect to the risks they face (Weinstein, 1989). Indeed, DeBondt and Thaler (1995) assert that "Perhaps the most robust finding in the psychology of judgment is that people are overconfident." But not our CEOs and entrepreneurs, at least according to the CEOs themselves.

The founding entrepreneurial CEOs also confessed that they are more likely than the non-founding CEOs to overemphasize first impressions of a situation or person and their own personal contacts with that situation or person. They also are somewhat more likely to report that they may tend to overemphasize their own impact on a situation or person. Langer (1975) was among the first to point out this putative bias. However, our CEOs as a group do not believe they are guilty of these biases.

Our CEOs also generally do not believe they overemphasize the importance of small risks. There is little difference between the founders and non-founders on this question.

The mean Likert Scale responses of the entire group of CEOs to the seven statements in Table 5.4 ranged between 2.88 and 3.59, effectively straddling the area between "agree" and "disagree." One can read such responses in several ways, but it is evident such numbers do not provide much support for the notion that most CEOs recognize in themselves the commonplace perceptual errors highlighted by behavioral finance. This is despite the fact that these errors have been repeatedly documented both for the general population and for business leaders in rigorously controlled tests.

Of course, it is possible that our CEOs are correct in their self-estimations and really do not fall prey to such perceptual distortions. We are strongly inclined to reject that supposition, but it is a possibility.

A CEO in our sample who leads a large corporation that he did not found, pithily observed that "Those guys [the founding CEOs] are full of themselves. They always think they have information other people don't, some sort of special touch, an unusual ability to persuade people, or a rare talent to size up other people very quickly. It just isn't so, but they have huge egos and receive so much attention that they convince themselves that they are masters of the universe, a kind of managerial superman." Our results provide at least modest support for this point of view. Founding CEOs do appear to be somewhat more susceptible than non-founding CEOs to what some observers label as irrationalities, but others simply classify as perceptual distortions.

Even so, the entrepreneurial CEOs in our sample seemed to be able to overcome these problems. As a group, they performed extremely well despite these distortions, if firm growth and profit rates are the guide. However, to be more definitive in this regard, we would need to have in our sample a very generous number of entrepreneurs who failed and went out of business. The perceptual distortions of *these* individuals may indeed have been fatal to them and their fledgling businesses. As it stands, about 20 percent of the CEOs in our sample at some time founded a business that failed (not necessarily their current business). It is worth noting that the responses of the "sometime failed" CEOs did not different significantly from those of rest of the CEOs.

Still, like Sherlock Holmes' dog that didn't bark, we must be cognizant of CEOs who are not in our sample because they failed and disappeared. It's plausible a large sample of failed CEOs might tell us that after the fact, they realize they were overoptimistic and that they overemphasized their own impact on events. In fact, there has been very little reputable research in behavioral finance on "losers" and failures. Hence, we are reduced to noting that those CEOs in our sample who at some time failed did not respond differently than other CEOs.

Chapter 6

Entrepreneurs as Internationalists and Novelty Seekers

It is not possible for this nation to be at once politically internationalist and economically isolationist. This is just as insane as asking one Siamese twin to high dive while the other plays the piano.
— Adlai E. Stevenson, American Presidential Candidate, 1952, 1956

According to one recent study that used four approaches to measuring the gains from trade, the increase in trade since World War II has boosted U.S. annual incomes on the order of $10,000 per household.
— Ben Bernanke, Chairman of the Board of Governors of the Federal Reserve System, 2007

Globalization requires us to reinvent everything.
— Nicolas Sarkozy, President of France, 2007

The scientific evidence concerning the personality traits of entrepreneurial individuals that we described in Chapter 2 informs us that these individuals relish new experiences. Conversely, individuals who seek new experiences and appreciate novelty are much more likely to become entrepreneurs than other individuals.

International activities and international trade fall into the "different" category for most firms. Different laws, rules, regulations, customs, and even languages apply. A mountain state entrepreneur shook his head knowingly when he talked with us and observed that "I had to learn a very different way of doing business when we began to sell in Japan." He was delighted by the opportunity to stay overnight in a traditional Japanese ryokan inn and to sleep on a tatami mat. New and different was for him a good thing. Indeed, for more than a few entrepreneurs, different often is better.

Thus, it is not a surprise that entrepreneurs tend to place more emphasis upon international activities (including production and sales) than other CEOs, because for most, international activity is new and different. "I get a charge out of talking to someone in Bangalore about my software," admitted a technology entrepreneur who also was a visible extrovert, another personality trait common to many entrepreneurs. One of our entrepreneurs compared doing international business with completing a puzzle and noted that "It takes quite a bit of ingenuity, flexibility, perseverance and the ability to put things together to succeed internationally." International business, he said, had "a magnetic effect" upon him and he enjoyed the new challenges it generated.

Many entrepreneurs appear to regard international involvement on the part of them or their firms as interesting activity per se, whether or not it leads to sales. "I've always enjoyed traveling," observed an entrepreneur who grew up in the Middle West, "and I gain new perspective from my trips, even if they are only tourist trips." An entrepreneur who subscribes to the *Economist* in order to keep up with worldwide events also told us he listens to the BBC world news broadcast each day at noon. "The way they subtly insert their political views into the news is a bit off-putting to me, but their approach is a refreshing change of pace from our network news and I think it gives me a much better feel for international markets and stocks."

Whatever the stimulus for international travel, most of our CEOs, founders and non-founders alike, use their travel as an opportunity to visit firms in other countries, sample goods and services, get a line on their competitors, and evaluate different ways of doing things. "I didn't believe that comparison advertising was a very good idea until I saw what they are doing in England and Australia," said an entrepreneur. He continued, "Some of the ads where they compare one company against another are hilarious and really grab your attention. When I returned home, we began to do the same thing—and it worked."

For some CEOs, of course, international business activity is not the product of their thirst for novelty and instead reflects hard calculations. A founding entrepreneur who sells specialty food products commented, "There are about 300 million mostly well fed people in the United States, more or less, but there are several billion hungry people living outside our borders. We would be foolish not to attempt to exploit international markets."

Table 6.1 CEOs, International Markets and International Trade

Characteristic	All sample CEOs	Founding CEOs	Non-founding CEOs	Statistical significance attached to difference
Am an internationalist	3.84	3.97	3.64	.083
Support NAFTA	3.10	3.75	2.59	.000
Regard outsourcing as a problem	2.76	2.47	3.24	.001
Company has offices outside the United States	4%	7%	1%	.029
Percentage of sales that is international	2.98%	3.88%	2.29%	.000

Travel to other countries is an important way in way in which entrepreneurs satisfy their global inclinations. Nevertheless, as one entrepreneur aptly put it to us, "Internationalization actually is an attitude and you don't have to travel to be interested in international production and sales, international events, and what's going on in other countries." In that vein, a non-founding CEO with international leanings noted that "You can sell internationally from the lawn chair in your backyard, if you really want to." This may be an exaggeration in many industries, but his point was that the Internet now enabled him to sell all over the world as well as in locations he hadn't even dreamed about previously.

COMPARING FOUNDING ENTREPRENEURS WITH OTHER CEOs

Table 6.1 helps us sketch the difference between founding entrepreneurial CEOs and other, non-founding CEOs insofar as international attitudes and issues are concerned. Interestingly, setting their behavior aside, both types of CEOs tend to regard themselves as internationalists in terms of their outlooks, though founding CEOs tend to do so slightly more often.

Free Trade and Outsourcing: A Telling Division of Views

It is concrete international issues and actions that clearly draw the line between entrepreneurs and other CEOs. For example, do our CEOs support NAFTA (North American Free Trade Agreement), a pact that always has attracted controversy? Entrepreneurial CEOs are much more likely to do so, and other CEOs actually tend to oppose it even though it has been a watershed international economic issue. Warned an entrepreneur who founded a company that supplies construction materials, "We can't shut the door on Mexico and Latin America without paying a price." One could conclude that his attitude on this issue is self-serving in that more than one-quarter of all American construction workers are immigrants, legal and illegal. Arguably, his business prospers when borders are open. However, when confronted with that notion, he argued against it, saying that he was in competition with Mexican suppliers of construction materials and therefore he wasn't certain whether open borders were good or bad for him personally.

Many entrepreneurs mirrored the construction material supplier's attitudes. "It's the survival of the fittest and I can compete with anyone," asserted an almost strident entrepreneur, while another, sounding almost like a page from an economics textbook, suggested, "Ultimately, it all comes down to our ability to make high-quality products at a competitive price. This requires me to have smart workers and some ingenuity. The alternative for us as a country is protectionism, higher prices, and a lower standard of living." Yet another entrepreneur remembered, "My grandfather came from Belgium almost one hundred years ago, didn't speak any English, and had to scramble to eat, but eventually made it. I don't see how I can in good conscience tell the latest wave of immigrants that they shouldn't have much the same chance."

Despite these views, some entrepreneurs and a larger proportion of non-entrepreneurial CEOs favored significant immigration restrictions. "How can we decide who should be in this country if we can't control our own borders?" offered a CEO who favored immigration restrictions. "We're in danger of losing the English language," cautioned an entrepreneur whose business was located on a city block that increasingly featured signs in Spanish.

Related to this, our entrepreneurial founding CEOs were less likely to regard outsourcing (the transfer of productive activities overseas, typically for cost reasons) as a significant problem. A high-technology CEO rose in his chair when he pointed out to us with a degree of passion that "People don't seem to understand the other side of the coin, which is 'in-sourcing.' Every day we deal with foreign firms that have established sites and offices here. They bring us business. It's nonsense to contend that we can get away with accepting investments here, but at the same time forbid investments abroad." If there is a unifying principle among the entrepreneurs who did not regard outsourcing of activities as a problem, it is that they view it as a rational, cost-minimizing way to do business that enables them to produce their products at a lower price. "I'll stop outsourcing the day after I see consumers boycotting Wal-Mart because it sells clothing from Malaysia and shoes from the PRC [People's Republic of China]," advised an entrepreneur, who at the same time said that both insourcing and outsourcing were efficiency driven.

To be fair, some non-entrepreneurial CEOs took the same side on the outsourcing question, but they were much less likely to do so. A representative non-founding CEO told us, "I think outsourcing is OK, but it is unpopular and besides, I can't always control what goes on over there" (referring to a factory his own company operates in Thailand). When asked if he was going to sell this operation or close it, he responded, "No, but I don't talk about it much."

All things considered, it would be a misrepresentation to say that all entrepreneurs are robust free traders who always support globalization. Nevertheless, it is accurate to say that the typical entrepreneur is much more likely to believe in and defend free trade (and the absence of tariffs and other trade protectionist activities) than the typical non-entrepreneurial CEO, who tends to be a risk-averter.

There is less certainty attached to free trade than to anti-free trade protectionism. Consistent with their frequent disdain for situations involving unpredictable flux and change, non-entrepreneurial CEOs often prefer certainty over the possibility that free trade might increase their prosperity. Our contention, based upon the data we have just presented here and our survey of behavioral genetics evidence, is that genetics have much to do with the lack of support of non-founding managerial CEOs for free trade. The twin and adoption studies we reviewed in Chapter 2 tell us that most, if not all, behavioral characteristics are heritable to some degree. We believe that a CEO's internationalist views and their support of free trade are a function of clearly heritable personality traits such as openness to new experiences, extraversion, and the willingness to incur risk. Hence, there is a genetic basis for the preference of entrepreneurs for free trade and international activities.

THOMAS JEFFERSON ONCE OBSERVED THAT "MERCHANTS HAVE NO COUNTRY."

Our CEOs did not portray this non-chauvinistic view to us, or at the very least if they maintained such a view, they hid it well. Virtually every CEO we interviewed perceived international trade as a means to benefit their company, their employees, their stockholders, and their country. Indeed,

> our entrepreneurs often expressed the view that it was their patriotic duty to sell abroad. This is consistent with their somewhat more conservative political views.

Against this, one might easily argue that individuals are not born free traders and that instead some free traders are "made" by instruction in an economics course. One of the authors of this book is an economics professor who would like to believe he has an impact in the classroom on such issues. Even so, it is apparent that the propensity of students and entrepreneurs to be attracted by situations involving novelty and risk is at work, both for entrepreneurs and for students. Free trade promises rewards, but brings with it risk and uncertainty that is attractive to some but repellant to others.

In Chapter 3, we found that non-founding, non-entrepreneurial CEOs, as a group, prefer certain outcomes over uncertain outcomes that they know ultimately would yield a higher average return. In other words, they are willing to sacrifice profit in order to reduce risk. This is not an irrational point of view. It is, however, a point of view that tends not to be associated with entrepreneurial activity. As a consequence, it is not an Olympian leap to conclude that many protectionists literally are born with the risk-averting fear of the unknown traits that lead them to prefer tariffs and similar change-reducing trade restrictions. Similarly, many (though not all) free traders are hardwired at birth with the traits that lead them to prefer the risks and rewards associated with free trade. Many entrepreneurs, then, appear to be born with their preferences for internationalism and free trade.

Principles into Action

If CEOs are internationalists and believe in free trade, then a variety of ways exist for them to put those principles into action. Table 6.1 reveals that the companies of our entrepreneurial CEOs are four times as likely as those of non-founding CEOs to have offices outside of the United States. In addition, the firms of our entrepreneurs earn a higher percent of their sales from international sources.

An entrepreneurial CEO who founded a software firm told us of the trepidation he had about opening an office in Frankfurt, Germany. "I thought I could sell in Europe, but I simply didn't know the first thing about how to do it. I didn't speak German and never had been to Germany. But I began to read, talked to some people, eventually signed up a representative, and opened our office. It was tough going for a year or so, but then things took off and now we are selling $5.3 million a year in Europe. It was a leap of faith that paid off."

The previous quotation in some ways summarizes the nature of the entrepreneurial experience. Some individuals instinctively forge ahead in such circumstances, while others quiver and withdraw. Entrepreneurs are different from other CEOs. Their differentially large tendency to engage in international production and sales provides additional evidence of the distinctive personality traits that motivate them.

ISSUES RELATING TO IMMIGRANTS AND IMMIGRATION

Many of the classic entrepreneurial success stories in the United States involve immigrants. An immigrant comes to the United States with not much more than a T-shirt on his back and subsequently makes his fortune. For example, perhaps one-third to one-half of all motel rooms in the United States are owned by someone with the last name of Patel. Virtually every Patel has emigrated directly from the Indian state of Gujarat, or comes to the United States after an intermediate stop in East Africa. Gujarati Patels, most of whom were not wealthy, are famous for purchasing down-at-the-heels motel properties, upgrading them, and turning a tidy profit while doing so. Impressively, they have faced and overcome blatant discrimination while achieving their successes.

Or, consider Andy Grove, the former chairman and CEO of Intel Corporation, who was born in Hungary. When he was twenty, he and his family fled Hungary at night in 1956 during the popular uprising that was brutally suppressed by the Soviets. By 1963, he had earned a PhD in Chemical Engineering from the University of California at Berkeley, and by 1979 was Intel's president.

Do individuals such as the Patels and Andy Grove represent a particularly healthy strain of entrepreneurial talent that has been self-selected by the process of immigration? That is, has the very act of their willingness to immigrate to a strange land marked them as risk-takers who are much more likely to possess and exhibit entrepreneurial characteristics? This argument seems plausible, and Gartner (2005, 2006) has formally described it as follows:

America is an amazing natural experiment—a continent populated largely by self-selected immigrants. All these people had the get-up-and-go to pull up stakes and come here, a temperament that made them different from their friends and relatives who stayed home. Immigrants are the original venture capitalists, risking their human capital—their lives—on a dangerous and arduous voyage into the unknown. (Gartner, 2006)

Approximately 11 percent of the CEOs in our sample immigrated to the United States and almost three-quarters of these individuals were founding entrepreneurs. This appears to support the Gartner hypothesis. However, large-sample evidence summarized by Shane (2008) indicates that immigrants are no more likely to start a new business than anyone else in the United States. Further, Shane asserts that census data indicate that there is no statistical relationship between the frequency of new business startups by immigrants in the United States and the frequency of business startups in those immigrants' home countries.

The tension between these two points of view illustrates a conflict between casual empirical observation and empirical research—not an unusual situation in the social sciences. A condition that appears to be true when one informally eyeballs a situation does not always remain true when large samples are taken and appropriate statistical controls are invoked. Casual observations can lead to faulty generalizations and even to erroneous stereotypes. On the other hand, sometimes the emperor actually does turn out to have no clothes. On occasion, shoddy, large-sample empirical work does not stand up to the harsh, practical light of day and even untrained eyes can see that a hypothesis does not conform to the real world.

Whichever the case here, the "Patel phenomenon" (one Patel was in our sample) suggests that significant differences may exist among immigrant ethnic groups insofar as entrepreneurial inclinations are concerned. One final point needs to be made in passing, however. While Andy Grove became very well educated and situated himself in the technological hotbed of Silicon Valley, in general the Patels have not been comparably well educated and also have spread out across the entire United States. "I could count on one hand the number of original Patels that have an M.B.A. degree," commented a Gujarati who came to the United States in the 1970s. Hence, this particular group of immigrants has not appeared to have needed anything more than their seemingly intrinsic strong motivation and personality traits in order to establish successful new businesses.

RELATED ISSUES

There are several related strategies that CEOs who are attracted by novelty and risk-taking can pursue that do not directly involve internationalism. A prime example is a CEO's support of research and development (R&D)

Table 6.2 Novelty and Risk-Taking at Home

Characteristic	All sample CEOs	Founding CEOs	Non-founding CEOs	Statistical significance attached to difference
Percentage of salesspent on research and development	4.91%	6.37%	3.79%	.028
Company has strong interest in intellectual property	53.4%	58.9%	49.2%	.033
Company partners with universities	55%	74%	41%	.000

expenditures. Table 6.2 reports that firms led by founding entrepreneurs spend a considerably higher proportion of their sales on R&D.

How is R&D activity connected to our previous discussions concerning entrepreneurial personalities? Research and development expenditures typically are quite risky. They may lead to multimillion dollar payoffs, or they may produce nothing but draining cash outflows. In the area of pharmaceuticals, for example, the rule of thumb is that fewer than one in ten experimental compounds eventually leads to a marketable drug that brings in sales revenues.

A gregarious entrepreneur portrayed his company's R&D activity to us this way: "I've always been willing to take a flyer on ideas that seem promising and our research and development activity probably falls into this category. We strike out a lot, but we've also come up with a dozen or so patents and perhaps half that many new products based upon our research. I'd estimate that about 20 percent of our revenues now come from our own research and development."

Like international activity, R&D expenditures require a CEO who is willing to take risks and who is attracted by novelty. Once again, scientific evidence suggests that these are heritable personality traits. Further, the data in Table 6.2 reveal an obvious dichotomy between entrepreneurial founding CEOs and the other CEOs insofar as R&D activity is concerned. This does not by itself prove that some CEOs are born with R&D instincts, but it encourages that notion.

One can also see in Table 6.2 that the firms led by entrepreneurial CEOs are more actively involved with intellectual property (IP), which is intangible, less predictable, and less susceptible to straight-forward ownership and control. One of the entrepreneurial CEOs in our sample leads a software firm whose sales have been diminished by IP thieves who often are located in the Pacific Rim. These miscreants illegally break the copy protection on the firm's software, copy it, and then use it themselves for nothing, or more likely sell it at low prices on the street. "Someone always is attempting to rip off our IP," lamented an entrepreneur. "We put millions of dollars into a product and then someone steals it for nothing." Despite this, he avowed that "IP is our life stream. It's risky, but absolutely necessary business for us. We try to stay a step ahead of these pirates."

Our point is not that ordinary CEOs do not hold the same views or on occasion act in the same fashion as entrepreneurial CEOs. Instead, it is that entrepreneurial CEOs think and behave differently where IP is concerned.

As was true for international production and sales, IP activity by a firm requires a CEO who can cope with risk and who is constitutionally able to deal with "striking out five times in a row" (the language of an entrepreneur). We submit both that entrepreneurs tend to be generously endowed with these traits and that these traits have substantial heritability. Born, not made, once again.

Finally, one can also see in Table 6.2 that entrepreneurs are much more likely to strike up partnership relationships with universities. The connections between universities and high-technology firms in Silicon Valley and elsewhere have been documented repeatedly. Of course, most firms do not operate in the realm of high technology. Even so, 74 percent of our entrepreneurial CEOs reported they have partnered with universities in some fashion, though only 41 percent of non-founding CEOs indicated the same.

"Partnering" here usually does not refer to joint R&D activity, but rather to diverse other university activities such as workforce development, executive training, provision of preventive health services by nursing students, affirmative action seminars, etc. Based upon conversations with our non-founding CEOs, we are inclined to believe that their firms had far more partnerships and relationships with universities (the term "university" here includes all post-secondary education, including community colleges) than they appeared to know about.

The non-founding CEOs were somewhat more insular in their approach to their work. Partnerships with local institutions of higher education often were not a high agenda item for them. They viewed their local institutions of higher education as resources "that are here" (the words of a CEO) and assumed that their employees "take advantage of them" (the view of another CEO), but these relationships were not something they felt required cultivation or specific attention. Opined yet another non-founding CEO, "We pay for the tuition of employees who earn a B or better on a course and nearly everyone knows this. It all happens almost automatically and really doesn't require much oversight from me."

Entrepreneurial CEOs as a group were a bit more comfortable with college professors than the other CEOs. "I enjoy getting together with those guys [college professors] and batting things around. I hire some of them as consultants from time to time," remarked a CEO who founded a manufacturing firm that has grown to approximately 500 employees.

We believe the university relationship results in Table 6.2 support the hypothesis that entrepreneurial founding CEOs instinctively are more open to new experiences that take form in higher education environments that often cannot easily be controlled by CEOs. Universities, after all, have been known to operate by rules that are antithetical to those honored by profit-making enterprises. Still, we caution that it does appear that the firms of the non-founding, non-entrepreneurial CEOs actually maintained more relationships with institutions of higher education than they were aware of when we solicited their views. However, such associations were a lower priority for the non-founding CEOs and so their higher education connections did not immediately come to their minds when we queried them.

CONCLUDING REMARKS

We already have seen that several of the personality traits associated with entrepreneurs, notably their tendency to be attracted by novelty and change, their extroversion, and their willingness to assume risk, are heritable characteristics. Now we can distinguish several of the ways that these traits are manifested in the behavior of entrepreneurial CEOs.

While entrepreneurs may not see internationalism and international trade as exotic activities, they do perceive them as being out of the ordinary and for that reason attractive. And, out of the ordinary experiences are things that most entrepreneurs instinctively crave. One east coast entrepreneur verbalized this to us: "If I had wanted an ordinary life, I would have gone to work for the Social Security Administration. I wanted something different and here I am." (He founded several biomedical firms and initially most failed, before achieving success.)

Analogously, entrepreneurs appear to perceive their R&D activities, their work in intellectual property, and their connections to universities as out-of-the-ordinary undertakings. Consequently, they are more willing to venture into the unknown and to take risks.

We argue that these "reaching out to the unfamiliar" behaviors are not randomly distributed among CEOs. Instead, these activities and the personality traits that generate them are concentrated among entrepreneurs. Once again, we observe that entrepreneurs constitute a different breed.

Chapter 7

CEOs and Their Boards

I realize that having a board of directors is a good thing for me and the firm, but a couple of my board members have foolproof ways of aggravating me.

—An entrepreneurial CEO in our sample (2005)

Boldness in business is the first, second, and third thing.

—Thomas Fuller, *Gnomologia* (1732)

... the devil's advocate may be the biggest innovation killer in America today. What makes this negative persona so dangerous is that it is such a subtle threat. Every day, thousands of great new ideas, concepts, and plans are nipped in the bud by devil's advocates.

—Tom Kelley, *The Ten Faces of Innovation* (2005)

One of singing legend Bob Dylan's more vivid contributions is the tune "You Gotta Serve Somebody." In this ditty, Hibbing, Minnesota's most famous product advises his listeners that all individuals ultimately are responsible to someone else, whether they are an ambassador, a politician, or a policeman. Even the high and mighty, he sings, ultimately have a superior. So also it is with our CEOs, most of whom (85 percent) have a board to which they report.

Needless to say, despite the reality that most CEOs have boards to which they report, that doesn't imply all of them necessarily enjoy their relationships with those boards, or that they even like having a board in the first place. As we shall see, entrepreneurial CEOs often find that their board relationships limit their behavior, much more so than managerial, non-founding CEOs. Despite this, and even though they founded their firm, 72 percent of entrepreneurs have a board that at least in theory has the legal ability to hire and fire them.

In some cases, the board of directors of an entrepreneur's company may not actually be independent. Family members and even subordinate employees may hold a majority of the seats on the board. Further, in some cases, an entrepreneur's board isn't actually a board of control; it is an advisory board that ultimately has little or no legal authority.

Firms led by non-entrepreneurial, managerial CEOs nearly always have boards that exercise legal authority over the firm. Entrepreneurs who own their own firm often have no legal need to establish a board; however, with increasing frequency, they find they must establish an independent board in order to attract the outside venture capital they believe they need. Venture capitalists and angel investors often insist upon the creation of a board and in other cases, banks and financial institutions may require the establishment of a board as a condition of their providing a loan to the entrepreneur. Any of these parties may demand and receive one or more positions on the entrepreneur's board of directors in recognition of their investments.

It's at this point that board operations may become exciting and unpredictable. The nature of many venture capitalists and financial angels who fund entrepreneurs is that they share many entrepreneurial personality characteristics. They usually are highly intelligent, energetic, motivated, sometimes impatient, and often strong-willed individuals with egos. Their past successes frequently lead them to the conclusion that their personal view of the world is precisely on target and therefore their vision for the entrepreneur's firm is superior to any other. Sometimes this even leads them to press the entrepreneur to relinquish some or all of the reins of management to experienced, non-entrepreneurial managers. This can be especially galling to entrepreneurs whose personal bodies and souls are tied up in their companies.

A well-known example involves Steve Jobs, one of the founders of Apple Computers. In 1985, he lost a power struggle with the Apple board of directors and resigned from the firm's management. Ironically, in 1997, he returned to Apple after it purchased NeXT, a computer platform development firm that Jobs founded after he left Apple. Jobs has been Apple's CEO ever since.

Yet, it is not always venture capitalists and financial angels who end up taking positions on an entrepreneur's board. A distinctive case involves an entrepreneur who engineered the takeover of an industrial firm that had a strong union that previously had reluctantly accepted wage and benefit concessions in order to save jobs. The union took two slots on the firm's board as partial compensation for its concessions and owned approximately 20 percent of the firm's stock. Hence, it was a big player.

The entrepreneur could not have achieved success in this takeover except for the strong and visible support of the firm's large and powerful labor union, which turned thumbs down on other takeover possibilities. The experience and motivation of the two union representatives, both of whom had long and sometimes contentious backgrounds as workers and union negotiators, contrasted visibly with backgrounds and motives of the remainder of the board members, whose experience spanned corporate management, finance, and similar ventures. Board meeting dynamics demonstrated that there is more than one way to acquire and interpret information about the world.

What's the lesson here? The upshot is that when a collection of the diverse individuals take seats in the same boardroom, there is the potential for fireworks and opposing views about future courses of action. "One of my board members asked me what I had been smoking," chuckled a successful entrepreneur who told us he inspired this comment after he had just presented a bold plan for the future to his board. For this and other reasons, many entrepreneurs disdain board members who question their actions, demand evidence, examine corporate travel and executive expenditures, or even doubt the major directions of the firm.

BOARD CULTIVATION AND THE EXERCISE OF POWER

The upshot of the circumstances cited above help explain why some entrepreneurs either have not established a board or have established a board under conditions that render it tame. "If I have to have one of those things," chortled a founding entrepreneur, "then I need to have control over it."

When meaningful boards do exist, skilled, savvy entrepreneurs devote considerable time to cultivating the members of these boards and to explaining their vision for the firm to them. This occurs both inside and outside of board meetings. Over time, proficient CEOs usually garner their board members' support for their vision. Bluntly put, accomplished, confident, and proficient CEOs frequently are capable of co-opting their boards (an observation to which a hearty majority of the CEOs we interviewed agreed). Capable, perhaps wily, CEOs bring into their camp even those board members who have been cynical or in opposition. Skillful CEOs end up having strong board support, as a consequence are well compensated, and are easily recognized as being in charge even though the board itself holds the formal levers of power. One CEO put it this way: "Yes, they have the power to fire me, but no, they're quite unlikely ever to do so because I keep them informed, respond quickly to their questions, and to be honest, play to their vanities. These things seem to be more important than the performance of our firm."

How are many CEOs able to place themselves in such an unassailable, powerful position? This is a question that ultimately addresses the question—how does one effectively exercise executive power and convince other individuals (especially board members) to take actions that they would not have taken otherwise? We have written extensively on this issue (Fisher and Koch, 1996) and offer a very brief summary here.

The four major tools enabling the exercise of leadership power are (1) coercion and rewards, (2) the use of formal structures and activities that elevate the CEO and grant her legitimacy, (3) expertise, and (4) charisma. Coercion, punishments, and rewards can force changes in behavior, but do not necessarily engender agreement or happiness. Wise CEOs do not overuse these tools, though we do not deny that they have both a place and effectiveness, particularly in authoritarian societies that do not follow the rule of law.

CEO legitimacy is often ignored but is vitally important, and it is boards that usually grant the tools of legitimacy even though these same tools ultimately often end up being used by CEOs in their relationships with their boards. What is legitimacy and what things make a CEO legitimate? Legitimacy is the recognition of position and place; these things usually are supplied by a board. Defined reporting relationship and authority, executive titles, offices, and perquisites can have the same effects on behavior and respect as clerical collars for clergy and academic regalia for college presidents, provided such things are not overused or abused.

Most important, however, is the clear and unmistakable assignment of appropriate power and responsibilities to CEOs by their boards. The very organization of board meetings, the arrangement of seats, and who is seen to be in charge often signals the position, power, and authority of the CEO. Board members who seek a powerful, effective, transformational CEO are wise to respect lines of authority and except in emergency circumstances avoid undermining CEOs by going behind their backs. Similarly, they must avoid obsessive micromanagement. If employees come to believe that the board actually is managing the firm, not their CEO, then they will behave accordingly and the CEO will become a eunuch. Boards, then, must provide their CEOs with sufficient authority to get the job done, even while they demand accountability. This is not an easy mixture to attain given the driving, almost hypomanic personalities of entrepreneurial CEOs and the individuals who often constitute their boards.

Expertise is almost self-explanatory. CEOs who clearly know what they are doing, who are in command of data, and who obviously know their ways around are CEOs who have a leg up on the exercise of power. The demonstration of expertise, both in structure and unstructured situations, is impressive to board members and employees alike. One CEO in our sample holds a one-hour meeting of all his firm's employees once per month, at which time he makes a presentation and invites questions, some of which he notes, *"are off the wall."* *"But,"* he commented, *it keeps me in touch and it demonstrates I am in control and know what's going on."*

DO CHARISMATIC CEOs PERFORM BETTER THAN OTHER CEOs?

The evidence is mixed. Are entrepreneurial, founding CEOs more charismatic than managerial, non-founding CEOs? There is only limited evidence here, but our interviews strongly suggest that the passion and drive of entrepreneurs provide them with generous amounts of charisma.

Charismatic leaders inspire trust and confidence. Historically, individuals such as George Washington, Thomas Jefferson, Presidents Teddy and Franklin Delano Roosevelt, Martin Luther King, Jr., and even less-admirable leaders such as Adolf Hitler and Benito Mussolini have radiated charisma and inspired their followers to support and action. Contemporary leaders such as Herb Kelleher, the founder of Southwest Airlines, and former General Electric CEO Jack Welch (not a founder) have had the same ability. The sincerity, energy, wisdom, courage, vision, and sensitivity of these leaders supercharge their subordinates (and even their board members). It is instructive that a board member we interviewed told us, "I'd go to the wall for that guy" (his CEO).

Employees and board members alike enthusiastically identify with CEOs who exhibit charisma, which frequently is the most effective way to influence behavior. Once on the CEO's team, board members boast about him, embrace his vision, compensate him well, and attempt to ensure he will not depart. On occasion, however, this charisma can be counterproductive because it is so powerful that it can blind board members and key employees to the mistakes of CEOs. Several of the most disastrous corporate CEO leadership failures in the past decade (Enron, Tyco, WorldCom) have occurred because co-opted boards were overwhelmed by CEO charisma

Table 7.1 The CEOs and Their Boards

Characteristic	All sample CEOs	Founding CEOs	Non-founding CEOs	Statistical significance attached to difference
My company doesn't have a board	15.4%	28.4%	5.3%	.000
Cultivate my board consistently	3.79	4.10	4.55	.000
Have the strong support of my board	3.50	4.36	2.84	.000
Have much to do with the selection of my board	3.32	4.21	2.64	.000
Believe strong boards discourage risk-taking	3.43	3.90	3.05	.000
Am both CEO and board chairman	46%	63%	34%	.000

and failed to exercise their responsibilities. CEO charisma caused them to overlook, or even ignore, signs contrary to their CEOs' enthusiastic, optimistic, but deceptive messages.

A LOOK AT OUR DATA

Table 7.1 discloses that 28 percent of the companies of founding CEOs and five percent of the companies of non-founding CEOs don't have a board to which they are responsible. Nevertheless, when they do have a board, our founding, entrepreneurial CEOs are much more likely to exercise power over the membership of their boards and to cultivate the members of their boards consistently. This latter result may surprise some but speaks of the more impersonal relationship non-founding CEOs have with their boards. They are managers, not founders, and are subtly less tied to this particular firm and its board members.

Founding CEOs also are much more likely than the others to believe they have the strong support of their board. Presumably this reflects both the fact that they have much to do with the composition of their boards and the time they spend cultivating and communicating with those boards. An entrepreneurial CEO described it this way: "This company is my life. No one gets on my board who isn't going to be helpful. I interact with them all the time."

Do strong boards cramp the style of CEOs and discourage risk-taking and entrepreneurship? Our founding CEOs are much more likely than the non-founding CEOs to hold that point of view. In light of our previous findings, this is not surprising. Entrepreneurs frequently have passionate, throbbing personalities that seem to inspire them to independent action, often against the customary flow. Hence, the more entrepreneurial a CEO, the more likely he is to sense that his board restricts his options and reduces his degrees of freedom. To the extent that founding CEOs are more entrepreneurial than the non-founding CEOs, they may be inclined to prefer decision-making freedom and either have no board or have a board that is effectively advisory.

More than a few entrepreneurs (those who founded their own firms) told us that they regretted that their boards tended "to meddle." A founding CEO expressed this feeling to us with this observation: "Board members are innately conservative and anyway, with all of the scandals that have occurred, they now think they have to show they're really doing something so they don't get sued." Another founding CEO opined candidly that "I try to ignore them as much as possible without causing problems."

Are boards helpful to entrepreneurs? The empirical evidence on this issue is mixed. Intelligent, supportive boards can be of great assistance to CEOs, especially those that have just started a firm and are in need of connections, wisdom, financing, and customers. An entrepreneurial CEO confessed to us that "My dream was hanging like a thin string until one of my board members convinced the bank to provide us with funding." Further, perceptive boards can reign in CEOs who embark on unwise courses of action. At the very least, board members can challenge the assumptions that underpin the CEO's actions. In the end, this is good mental exercise for most CEOs, because it forces them to sharpen their cases and justify what they are doing. Boards also usefully monitor and verify firms' financial performance (Sarbanes-Oxley has made a definite imprint here, according to the CEOs in our sample), evaluate the CEO, and determine their compensation. Recent corporate history suggests that some boards have failed to exercise their fiduciary responsibilities in this regard.

Against this, some boards attempt to micromanage and neuter their CEOs by constantly interfering in their legitimate bailiwicks. This is not an uncommon situation in academic institutions where boards can become dominated by alumni and individuals who have a pet concern (often intercollegiate athletics) that motivates their activity (see Fisher and Koch, 1996). But, our interviews and the data in Table 7.1 reveal that the same tendencies can be present on corporate boards.

The power of a CEO typically increases significantly when he or she is both the chief executive officer and the chair of the company's board. The board's chair is responsible for constructing meeting agendas and for communicating with board members. When one individual occupies both of these posts, the potential for good or evil increases significantly. Highly capable CEOs use this authority and freedom to push their company forward to even greater heights and therefore many covet this joint designation. Less capable CEOs, however, can use this power to obfuscate and deny legitimate board inquiries. Because the chair of the board does establish the agenda for board meetings, he or she has a major influence over the issues that eventually are considered by the board. Therefore, a devious combination chief executive officer/chair often can prevent questioning board members from having a major platform to state their concerns.

When the positions of chief executive officer and chair are combined, there also is a potential for the CEOs/board chair to feather their personal nests and those of her major subordinates with perquisites that may not be highly visible to board members. Indeed, two of the more candid CEOs we interviewed intimated to us that their boards "were not completely aware of the perks" they had accumulated.

In our sample, almost twice as many founding CEOs occupied both the chief executive officer and the board chair role as was true for non-founding CEOs. Did this make any difference in performance? In our sample, the firms of CEOs who occupied both posts grew faster and earned higher profit rates than the firms where the two posts were separate. Nationally, however, the empirical evidence on this issue is mixed. It is notable that most corporate governance and compensation experts advocate that the two posts be separated (Crystal, 1991) and that the same individual not occupy both.

CONCLUDING REMARKS

Opined one of our entrepreneurial CEOs to us, "The only reason I have a board is because I had no other choice; I needed money and free legal advice." These words from one of our entrepreneurs were echoed in essence by many others. Our study supports this position. Founding CEOs are less likely to have a board because they feel that entrepreneurial initiatives may be squelched or delayed by a control group. And, when they do have a board, it follows that founding CEOs, much more than non-founding CEOs, attempt to play a major role in the appointment of board members and they expect their strong support. Finally, out of the same need for initiative and dispatch, but contrary to conventional intelligence, a clear majority of founding CEOs plays the role of both chief executive officer and board chair. The bottom line is, founding CEOs prefer to be in charge.

Chapter 8

Are You an Entrepreneur?

Rain beats a leopard's skin, but it does not wash out the spots.

—Ashanti Proverb

Go and wake up your luck.

—Persian Proverb

Nothing will ever be attempted, if all possible objections must be first overcome.

—Samuel Johnson in *Rasselas*, 1759

In Chapter 3, we wrote: "The evidence . . . strongly suggests that if you enjoy stirring things up, frequently think outside the box, generate lots of innovative ideas, frequently violate the status quo, often violate the chain of command, and do not strongly believe in organizational structures, then you're much more likely to become an entrepreneur." We now can add to this—if you are risk-taker who often prefers uncertainty and an opportunistic state of flux to situations full of stability, then you're also more likely to become an entrepreneur.

Since behavioral genetics evidence indicates that these entrepreneurial characteristics appear to be heritable, this implies that some individuals are born with a predisposition to enjoy stirring things up and disturbing the status quo. Over time, our evidence suggests, a sorting process occurs and such individuals are more likely to move into entrepreneurial leadership positions.

A common reaction to the previous information, we have found, is for an individual to say, "That sounds like me, but how can I really be sure?" Unfortunately, we don't have the ability to be absolutely precise concerning the probability of someone being a good entrepreneur, or even an entrepreneur at all.

THE "AM I PREDISPOSED TO BECOME AN ENTREPRENEUR?" TESTS

What we have developed, however, are two tests, one shorter and one longer, that generally separate the wheat from the chaff where entrepreneurial tendencies of individuals are concerned. The first, the short test, consists of only twelve questions and should take you no more than ten minutes to complete. The second, the long test, probes much more deeply into the aspects of entrepreneurial behavior and personality. It will take thirty to forty minutes to complete.

The Short Test

Respond to the following statements using these indicators:

1 = I strongly disagree

2 = I disagree

3 = I am neutral

4 = I agree

5 = I strongly agree

1. I like to stir things up and promote change.
2. I frequently think outside the box and propose innovative solutions.
3. I don't mind violating the chain of command in order to get things done.
4. I don't believe in strong, hierarchical organizational structures; I prefer more flexibility in organizations.
5. I am often stimulated by new ideas, new people, and new situations.
6. I generate lots of innovative ideas.
7. I frequently violate the status quo.
8. I often become really passionate and excited about the things I do, but also have some low points as well.
9. I am rather ambitious.

10. Either my father or my mother, or both, were entrepreneurial people who often took risks.

11. Which of the following two choices do you prefer?

A: $1,000 with absolute certainty ($p = 1.00$)

B: $2,050 with a probability of one-half ($p = .5$) *and* $0 with a probability of one-half ($p = .5$)

"*p*" here represents the probability that the event will occur.

Thus, choice A means you will receive $1,000 with absolute certainty ($p = 1.00$), with no risk of default. Choice B, however, will provide you with $2,050 one-half the time ($p = .5$), but give you nothing the other one-half of the time ($p = .5$).

Respond with one of the following:

1 = I strongly prefer choice B.

2 = I prefer choice B.

3 = I'm indifferent; either choice is OK with me.

4 = I prefer choice A.

5 = I strongly prefer choice A.

12. Which of the following two choices do you prefer?

C: $1,000 with absolute certainty ($p = 1.00$)

D: $3,000 with a probability of one-half ($p = .5$) *and* -$600 with a probability of one-half ($p = .5$)

Choice C is identical to choice A in the previous problem; you always receive $1,000 without fail. Choice D, however, is more complex. One-half of the time, choice D produces a $3,000 gain for you, but the other one-half of the time, choice D involves a $600 *loss.*

Respond with one of the following:

1 = I strongly prefer choice C.

2 = I prefer choice C.

3 = I'm indifferent; either choice is OK with me.

4 = I prefer choice D.

5 = I strongly prefer choice D.

Interpreting Short Test Results

Have you made your choices? Let us see what your responses have to say about you and your entrepreneurial instincts.

On each of the first ten statements, current entrepreneurs and those who are most likely to become entrepreneurs choose higher numbered responses. That is, they are much more likely to choose option 4 or 5 as their response (I strongly agree, or I strongly prefer) than option 1 or 2 (I strongly disagree and I strongly prefer the opposite). Statements 1 through 7 replicate statements to which we asked our 234 CEOs to respond. On these first seven questions, the entrepreneurial CEOs, who had founded their own firm, averaged a 4.17 response, while the managers, the non-founding CEOs, averaged only 3.15.

Statements 8 and 9 were not administered to our 234-CEO sample, but reflect our interviews with the CEOs and our review of the literature. Entrepreneurial CEOs often become quite passionate and excited about their work (hyper, some would say) and not infrequently end up working very long hours because of their passion and excitement. If you did not respond with option 4 or 5 (I agree, or I strongly agree), then arguably you are unlike most of the founding entrepreneurs we encountered.

Statement 10 is a straightforward response to the scientific findings of behavioral genetics. If one or both of your parents were entrepreneurially inclined, then it appears that you are more likely to be entrepreneurially inclined than another otherwise identical individual. This reflects the fact that many entrepreneurial traits are at least partially heritable.

Statements 11 and 12 involve choice making in which the choice is binomial. One must choose either one or the other of the alternatives. There is no third choice. We reported in Chapter 3 that 79 percent of founding entrepreneurs preferred risky choice B, while only 43 percent of non-founding, managerial CEOs had the same preference. They preferred the certain but potentially less lucrative alternative A.

The same dichotomy appeared with respect to statement 12. Seventy-one percent of entrepreneurs preferred risky choice D, but only 32 percent of managers had that same preference. Once again, they preferred absolutely certain choice C.

What does this imply about your own entrepreneurial inclinations? If you chose both alternatives, A and C, then you don't fit into the usual entrepreneurial mold. This does not necessarily mean you cannot or will not become an entrepreneur, but it does suggest that you are less likely to do so. Arguably, it may also suggest that you may be less successful if you do choose to become an entrepreneur anyway because you shrink from taking the risks that usually characterize entrepreneurial activity.

Table 8.1 What Your Responses to the Eleven Entrepreneurial Questions Tell You about Your Entrepreneurial Tendencies

Result:	4.0 to 5.0 average on the first seven statements and you selected choices B and D (bonus if you responded with option 4 or 5 on statements 8 and 9 and have a parent who was an entrepreneur) *You appear to have strong entrepreneurial tendencies.*
Result:	3.0 to 3.99 average on the first seven statements and you selected choices B and D only once or not at all *You appear to have some entrepreneurial tendencies, but may not be ideally suited to become a successful entrepreneur.*
Result:	1.0 to 2.99 average on the first seven statements and you did not select either choice B or D *You appear to be rather unlikely to become an entrepreneur; perhaps this is a signal that you should think about other things.*

Comparing Your Short Test Results to Those of Our Entrepreneurs

Our experience with our 234 CEOs indicates that those whose average score is 4.0 or above are most likely to be entrepreneurial in their behavior. Those whose average score is below 3.0 are much more likely to be managers rather than entrepreneurs. Those individuals whose scores range between 3.0 and 4.0 have some entrepreneurial instincts, but the closer that score is to 3.0, the less likely they are to become entrepreneurs.

Only four of our 102 entrepreneurs scored below 3.0 on their responses to the first seven statements; more than fifty of our 132 managers (non-founding CEOs) did so. Further, only three managers (non-founding CEOs) scored above 4.10, while almost two-thirds of our founding CEOs, our entrepreneurs, scored above 4.10.

Table 8.1 summarizes the information provided by the entrepreneurial statements and what both our sample of 234 CEOs and behavioral genetics evidence suggest with respect to your predisposition to become an entrepreneur.

The Long Test

Answer Yes or No to these questions; circle the answer given if it coincides with yours.

1. Have you ever put your job on the line?   Yes
2. Have you ever resigned in frustration?   Yes
3. Have you ever failed?   Yes

4. Are you adventurous?   Yes

5. Do you tend to be politically liberal?   No

6. Are you involved in community activities?   Yes

7. Are you a member of a religious organization?   Yes

8. Do you attend a religious institution?   Yes

9. Would you serve in the military in a national emergency?   Yes

10. Are you married to your first spouse?   Yes

11. Have you traveled abroad?   Yes

12. Have you initiated a business or businesses?   Yes

13. Are you intimately involved with business associates?   No

14. Are you an introvert?   No

15. Do you easily get bored?   Yes

16. Are you often viewed as a loner?   Yes

17. Do you enjoy stirring things up?   Yes

18. Should a board of directors govern a corporation?   No

19. Have you had more than three jobs in a ten-year period?   Yes

20. When you drive, do you always observe the speed limit?   No

21. Do you ever unfasten your seatbelt without permission?   Yes

22. Do you exercise?   Yes

23. Do you drink at business luncheons?   No

24. Are you a risk-taker?   Yes

25. Were either of your parents risk-takers?   Yes

26. Were your other close relatives risk-takers?   Yes

27. Was your education important in your business?   No

28. Have you been active in politics?   No

29. Would you run for office?   No

30. Do you like to be in charge?   Yes

31. Do you read for pleasure?   No

32. Do you read primarily professional publications?   Yes

33. Were you in the upper 10 percent of your secondary school class?   No

34. Did you participate in athletic activities?   Yes

35. Did you always want to be the leader?   Yes

36. Do you have close relationships with many people?   No

37. Are you sometimes moody?   Yes

38. Do you share your problems with others?   No

39. Is the right school important to you?   No

40. Did you work while in school?   Yes

41. Is loyalty as important as competence?   Yes

42. Do you always appear confident?   Yes

43. Have you coached your children in athletic activities?   Yes

44. Do some consider you arrogant?   Yes

45. Are you invariably optimistic?   Yes

46. Are you more conservative than liberal?   Yes

47. Do you adhere to your organization chart?   No

48. Do you stick to your plans?   No

49. Are you overconfident?   No

50. Do you have an abundance of energy?   Yes

51. Have you ever felt in danger?   Yes

52. Could you get along without a cell phone or Blackberry?   No

53. Do people think you are charming?   Yes

54. Are you politically independent?   Yes

55. Do you have a spontaneous sense of humor?   Yes

56. Should politics be used to advance your business?   Yes

57. Do you tend to buck the status quo?   Yes

58. Do you tend to disregard discouraging news?   Yes

59. Are you a Type A personality?   Yes

60. Are you passionate about your work?   Yes

61. Are you overweight?   No

62. Do you dress well?   No

63. Is the good opinion of others very important to you?   No

64. Do you believe in leadership by walking around?   Yes

65. Do you define yourself in terms of the bottom line?   No

66. Do you believe in a diverse work force?   Yes

67. Do you micromanage?   Yes

68. Do you typically speak before thinking?   Yes

69. Do you take criticism well?   No

70. Do you practice affirmative action?   No

71. Do you prefer a hierarchical organization?   No

72. Is merit pay important?   Yes

73. Is vision more important than mission?   Yes

74. Do you believe in team decision making?   No

75. Can entrepreneurialism be learned?   No

76. Did you bug your parents?   Yes

77. Were you achievement oriented in school?   No

78. Are you cool in a crisis?   Yes

79. Are you restless?   Yes

80. Are you generally happy?   Yes

81. Are good friends important to you?   Yes

Interpreting Your Long Test Results

Count up the number of answers circled.

70 and up = Entrepreneurial personality
60 to 70   = Entrepreneurially inclined
0 To 59 = Transactional personality and not entrepreneurially inclined

CAVEATS AND SOME ADVICE

No set of statements such as we have just developed is capable of determining absolutely who will, or will not, become an entrepreneur. Human behavior is far more complex than can be adequately represented in any set of statements or choices. We met several CEOs who did not score well on the short test, but nonetheless became entrepreneurs. Further, one of them became a very successful entrepreneur.

Even so, if on the short test you consistently provided responses 1, 2, or 3, and you preferred choices A and C rather than B and D, then the odds are against your becoming an entrepreneur, much less a successful one. Ditto if you scored below 60 on the long test. Recall our discussion of the height of National Basketball Association (NBA) players. If you stand less than 6′ in height, then the odds are stupendously high against your finding a spot on an NBA roster as a player. Highly unusual and exceptional individuals of short stature such as Calvin Murphy (5′9″) appear perhaps once a generation and subsequently make it in the NBA, but candor requires us to acknowledge that Mr. Murphy constituted almost a genetic aberration. He averaged almost 18 points per game in 14 seasons for the Houston

Rockets, an amazing performance in a league where the average player stood 6'6".

Hence, if your average response to the short test statements was below 3.00, and you also selected choices A and C, and you scored below 60 on the long test, then you must give serious consideration to whether you really are a Calvin Murphy type of individual who will defy the odds. Our advice for you is more opaque and less certain if your responses fell into the 3.0 to 4.0 bracket and you selected choice B or D on the short test, or if you scored between 60 and 70 on the long test. Perhaps you have what it takes, but you should consider your options carefully. Are you really cut out for the pressure and uncertainty that often accompanies entrepreneurial activity? Are you really attracted to situations that are in flux? Can you see yourself making decisions that could result in your own bankruptcy? If you are uncertain, or your answers to these questions are "No," then you should think twice about engaging in entrepreneurial activity. As one entrepreneur put it, "People like that should pay other people to take risks for them and take refuge in their government bonds and insurance policies." Harsh words, but probably wise.

DO ENVIRONMENT, EDUCATION, AND EXPERIENCE MAKE A DIFFERENCE?

If our tests show that you are not inclined to be an entrepreneur, but you would like to take the entrepreneurial plunge anyway, or you would like to make yourself a more successful entrepreneur, then what? Can you really improve your entrepreneurial chances by making "the right moves"? The answer is a qualified "yes," but we hasten to point out that you may be running uphill as you do so.

We have presented persuasive behavioral genetics evidence that much entrepreneurial activity is genetically determined, and we have supplemented those findings with supportive data from our CEO surveys. Nevertheless, not all behavior in the world is genetically determined. Heredity and environment interact to produce the behavior we actually observe. In the context of entrepreneurial activity, a variety of studies have demonstrated that environment, education, and experience all could make a difference. If you consistently associate with entrepreneurs, listen to them, and observe their actions and behavior, then you are more likely to become an entrepreneur yourself (one of the earliest of these studies in this vein is Freeman, 1986, while one of the most recent is Sorensen, 2007). Prior experience also appears to increase the probability that one will undertake an entrepreneurial venture (Cantner, Goethner, and Meder, 2007) and we already have cited evidence that entrepreneurial education appears to be associated with higher levels of entrepreneurial activity.

It is scientifically plausible that an individual's environment, education, and life experiences interact with heredity to generate more or less entrepreneurial activity. The major difficulty with evidence similar to that we have just cited is that it suffers from possible self-selection bias. This is the problem in a nutshell: individuals who by virtue of their genetic endowment and personality traits are more likely to become entrepreneurs are also more likely to associate with entrepreneurs, to pursue entrepreneurial education, and to have accumulated previous entrepreneurial experience. Hence, when we observe an individual entrepreneur who has been spending time with other entrepreneurs, has acquired entrepreneurial education, and who perhaps even has taken an entrepreneurial plunge in the past, is the person's future entrepreneurial activity due to these factors or instead due to genetic makeup? Do genetically inclined entrepreneurs naturally drift into these situations, which ultimately do not really change their innate desire to become entrepreneurs? Or, do these situations genuinely change individuals who otherwise would not have become entrepreneurs?

There is no doubt that it is difficult to separate these influences—to detach genetic influences from those that are primarily environmental. This is a perpetual problem in the social and behavioral sciences where public policy questions are concerned. Are the income differences we observe between individuals a function of their genetic endowments, or their environments, or a bit of both? Did Barack Obama and John McCain become presidential candidates because it was in their genes, or because of the people they hung around with and the education and experiences they accumulated earlier?

A variety of statistical adjustments can be introduced into analyses of entrepreneurial activity that attempt to eliminate self-selection bias. Even so, in the absence of knowing someone's precise genetic endowment, it is impossible to eliminate self-selection bias completely.

Therefore, as things presently stand, we cannot determine with precision the extent to which environment, education, and experience really make a difference. It seems plausible that such factors might make a difference in entrepreneurial activity because not all behavior is genetically determined and not all personality traits are heritable. Unfortunately, the evidence currently available to us does not allow us to confirm such a relationship.

However, there is another aspect to this discussion that we should not neglect. Even if one were to take the view that individual genetic endowments are the only thing that count in terms of stimulating individual entrepreneurial activity and behavior, then it still can be true that the factors just mentioned (environment, education, experience) might help an entrepreneur survive and become more successful. That is, given that I

have become an entrepreneur, how can I become a successful (more successful) entrepreneur? We believe it is silly to argue that knowledge of accounting and economics will not enable most individuals to become more successful entrepreneurs. It may be an arguable proposition whether environment, education, and experience are responsible for making someone an entrepreneur, but it is far less arguable that appropriate environments, education, and experience improve entrepreneurial survival and success. Thus, there is a role for business schools, entrepreneurial incubators, and mentors. Moreover, the school of hard knocks is hardly irrelevant to how entrepreneurs fare.

In the years to come, as genetic researchers make progress in identifying the precise nature of each individual's genetic endowment, no doubt it will be possible for us to disentangle the relationship between heredity and the various aspects of environment insofar as entrepreneurial behavior and activity are concerned. For now, however, we must be satisfied with observing that many, perhaps most, entrepreneurs appear to be born rather than made. Those who do not possess the personality traits that are fundamental to entrepreneurial activity battle against the odds, much as a 200-pound man must struggle to gain a position in the National Football League. It can and does happen, but it is not the most likely outcome.

FINAL THOUGHTS

It is commonplace in the United States for public-spirited individuals and school counselors to encourage individuals by telling them that they can achieve any goal if they are willing to work hard enough, long enough. We risk sounding like a modern incarnation of pessimistic philosopher Arthur Schopenhauer, or perhaps even Dickens's Ebenezer Scrooge, when we observe that often this is faulty advice.

Individuals are gifted in different ways. Some individuals are natural athletes, others can't dribble or hit a ball but are marvelously suited to acquiring a foreign language, constructing Internet Web pages, or building homes. Still other individuals are well suited to become entrepreneurs because they welcome change, think innovatively, are optimistic, driven, and relish risk-taking.

As a matter of wise public policy, we should permit individuals to pursue whatever their personal dream happens to be. Therefore, if an individual who averages a 2.0 response on our statements nonetheless wishes to become an entrepreneur, then he or she should be allowed to do so. Yet, the odds are against this intrepid individual and the evidence presented in this book explains why.

Many years ago, Grantland Rice, the famous twentieth-century sports writer, allegedly averred (and we paraphrase) that "the race doesn't always go to the swiftest, or the fight to the strongest, but that is the way to bet." So also it is with entrepreneurial activity. We now know well the personality traits that are associated with and promote entrepreneurship. You and I put ourselves at risk if we ignore this evidence.

Chapter 9

Finding the Right Leader: What Entrepreneurial Research Tells Us

Eagles don't flock—you have to find them one at a time.

—Ross Perot, 1930–

Entrepreneurs are simply those who understand that there is little difference between obstacle and opportunity and are able to turn both to their advantage."

—Niccolo Machiavelli, 1469–1527

I can save you some time and tell you what you ought to write in your book. Good leaders must be entrepreneurial. And, entrepreneurs make the best leaders.

—A CEO whom we interviewed for this study, 2006

We come now to the payoff. What can we do with the knowledge we have accumulated about entrepreneurs? Can we use it to improve the quality of organizational leadership?

First, let's review the bidding. Do successful CEOs tend to be entrepreneurial? We believe the preceding eight chapters have firmly established the inclination of successful CEOs to be entrepreneurial. The reverse, the data also suggest, is true as well. Skillful entrepreneurs tend to be successful CEOs.

Note that we don't argue that all successful CEOs are entrepreneurial, nor do we argue that every intrepid entrepreneur will become a successful CEO.

Instead, we assert that the evidence suggests that these things tend to be true. Once again, it is a matter of probabilities. If you want to hire a successful CEO, find an appropriately qualified individual who is entrepreneurial by nature.

Our previous research dealing with college presidents (Fisher and Koch, 2004) strongly encourages the conclusion that we can generalize our inferences to many different settings. Successful CEOs, whether they operate in corporate, government, military, or university environments, tend to be more entrepreneurial than less successful CEOs. The flexible, innovative, optimistic, and risk-taking nature of entrepreneurial leaders breeds success noticeably more often than what one of our CEOs labeled a "sit on your hands approach to management."

Both our survey evidence and our interviews provide firm support for the hypothesis that managers who embrace change and use it as a means to improve their organizations tend to be more successful than managers who fear change and conversely use their power to minimize the risks they face. Literally, many of these individuals believe they will make their own luck. They believe that fortune indeed favors the bold. If they weren't entrepreneurs, they might taste risk as a window-cleaner on a skyscraper, as a day trader, as a U.S. Marine in the Middle East, or as a policeman in a big city. Such individuals readily accept the challenges associated with risk-taking.

We hasten to note that risk-aversion has its place in management and finance and a CEO who did not attempt to avoid certain risks would qualify as irrational in most conventional economic and behavioral models. Those who invested in subprime mortgage financial packages in the middle of this decade found to their consternation that these subprime mortgage packages (labeled as *tranches*) carried with them far more risk than the investors had supposed and perhaps as well more risk than financial rating agencies detected. The result was pecuniary disaster for some of these investors and the highly public resignations of a half-dozen banking and finance CEOs.

Not every risk, then, is attractive. Nevertheless, the paramount characteristic separating successful, entrepreneurial CEOs from the rest is their willingness to assume intelligent risks. Entrepreneurial CEOs often put their own personal resources and reputations at risk. Many of these entrepreneurs actually relish the difficulties and impediments they encounter. They rise to the challenge. As one expressed it to us, "Generally the worse the circumstances, the better I like it. I know I can improve the situation and people are much more willing to let me take strong steps when things are going bad."

The previous quotation is revealing. This particular entrepreneur *knew* he could improve the situation. How he knew this, we're not quite certain, but like most entrepreneurs, he exuded confidence. Such individuals believe they have captured what a poet scenically described as "lightning's hour" (Day-Lewis, 1933, p. 37) and are uniquely situated to exploit the situation.

The reality is that most entrepreneurs are self-assured individuals who often have extraordinary faith in their own abilities. Alfred P. Sloan, Jr., founder of the firm that became General Motors, approached braggadocio when he asserted, "Take my assets—but leave me my organization and in five years I'll have it all back" (Sloan, 1925). In other words, do whatever you're going to do, and I'll still find a way to emerge successful.

Or, consider the example of Mike McGavick, who took over an almost bankrupt Safeco Insurance Company in 2001 and breathed life into it with a series of entrepreneurial initiatives mixed with cutting, pruning, and writing off unwise previous investments. Safeco's stock price tripled and he was justifiably regarded as a savior. Even so, more than a few observers told McGavick that he was crazy to attempt to turn around Safeco. Yet, he was not deterred.

Some entrepreneurial executives become serial specialists in Safeco-type turnarounds and bring their quintessential entrepreneurial characteristics to one organizational table after another (Slatter, Lovett, and Barlow, 2006). James and Craig Bouchard, brothers who lead the NASDAQ-listed firm Esmark, have acquired and turned around a dozen steel companies in an era when steel production and service have been shrinking in the United States. In the higher education arena, Scott Miller, currently the President of Bethany College in West Virginia, has dramatically improved the prospects of three very distinct collegiate institutions.

CHARACTERISTICS OF TURNAROUND EXECUTIVES

Slatter, Lovett, and Barlow (2006, p. 10) contend that executives that turn around organizations exhibit the following characteristics:

They quickly develop clear short-term priorities and goals.
They exhibit visible authority.
They set expectations and enforce standards.
They are decisive and implement their decisions quickly.
They communicate continuously with all stakeholders.
They build confidence and trust by being transparent and honest.
They adopt an autocratic leadership style during crisis stabilization.

> While some or all of these characteristics may describe portions of the activities of turnaround entrepreneurs (whether they operate in business, government, the military, or academe), we believe they have overlooked the most important characteristics—the willingness of turnaround CEOs to bear risks, their ability to innovate and to develop solutions that appear to many to be outside the usual conceptual boxes, their tendency to violate administrative and organizational hierarchies, their superb ability to motivate employees and constituents, and their own personal charisma. We argue that the evidence is clear—most turnaround entrepreneurs are born with these characteristics rather than acquiring them along the way and further that these characteristics are far more important to turnaround success than characteristics such as an autocratic decision-making style. Boards of directors that find themselves in need of a turnaround executive should keep this in mind when making appointments.

Turnaround entrepreneurs nearly always are intelligent, driven individuals with great energy and will power. They have the ability to see new ways of doing things and the optimism and courage to take steps that would cause most others to blanch. Repetitively, they move into situations that intimidate and baffle less determined and entrepreneurial individuals.

Of course, the great majority of the entrepreneurs we have examined weren't in the turnaround business. They founded their own businesses and committed their time and fortunes to that endeavor. They are epitomized by Jeff Bezos, the founding CEO of Amazon.com, who pursued his dream of an Internet supermarket store through almost a decade of red ink and the nitpicking of media naysayers and financial analysts. Tradition (probably apocryphal) has it that he developed his original business plan for Amazon while riding in a dented old Chevy Blazer from Texas to Washington State. Today's Amazon is experiencing booming sales. The firm is profitable and somewhat less entrepreneurial competitors such as Barnes and Noble wonder what move Bezos will make next. Bezos, hardly a shrinking violet, *knew* he could get the job accomplished.

Needless to say, not all entrepreneurs experience Amazon-like success. Witness the carnage of the dot.coms at the beginning of this decade. Nevertheless, one cannot escape the sense that typical entrepreneurs are as resolute as a missionary in believing in the content of their message and in their own eventual success. Like soldiers in a battle zone who fervently believe that it is the other guy who will be killed, new entrepreneurs typically believe that others may fall along the wayside, but they won't. Donald Trump, whose entrepreneurial instincts and self-confidence bulge from his very being, captured the supremely positive spirit of so many entrepreneurs when he said, "I'm not running for President, but if I did, I'd win" (Trump, 1987). One is reminded of the lyrics from the Broadway musical, "Annie Get Your Gun," in which Annie declares, "Anything you can do, I can do better" (Stlyrics, 2007). Many entrepreneurs appear to take these words to heart.

Risk-lovers and risk-averters, a literary take: Milo Minderbinder: *"I have a sure-fire plan for cheating the federal government out of six thousand dollars. We can make three thousand dollars apiece without any risk to either of us. Are you interested?"* Yossarian: *"No."* (Joseph Heller, *Catch-22*, 1961.)

WHERE DO THESE ENTREPRENEURIAL QUALITIES COME FROM?

The tenor of the scientific evidence that bears upon the source of entrepreneurial activity and personality characteristics is clear. Behavioral genetics research over the past few decades has pinpointed the connection of genetics to entrepreneurial personality traits. Personality traits such as openness to new experiences, receptivity to change, and willingness to assume risks have genetic bases and are heritable. Depending upon the trait, up to 65 percent of the appearance of that trait in an individual may be genetically determined.

Thus, when we observe the behavior and actions of individuals such as Jeff Bezos and Donald Trump, much of what we see in them is a function of their own genes. It seems highly probable they were born with their entrepreneurial inclinations.

We argue that most entrepreneurs are born, not made. An individual's home environment, education, and experience also contribute to his or her entrepreneurial activity, but are surprisingly less important than many initially believe. We conclude that doubters on this issue either have not yet examined the literature of behavioral genetics that bears on these issues, or simply find such evidence contrary to their prejudices. We include in this latter category a variety of individuals, ranging from leftist Marxist theorists who believe that experience and environment are everything, to much more politically conservative academics that teach entrepreneurship in our universities. The latter individuals not only believe that they can teach entrepreneurial principles effectively, but also that they can generate large numbers of entrepreneurs with their efforts. Once again, we feel obliged to stress that we aren't arguing that genetics is the entire game insofar as entrepreneurs are concerned. Environment, education, and experience do play roles. Instead, we underline the extent to which we are much more likely to be able to identify a successful CEO if we focus upon individuals who exhibit entrepreneurial personality traits.

ARE IMMIGRANTS MORE ENTREPRENEURIAL?

John Gartner, a Johns Hopkins University professor, argues that voluntary immigrants to the United States reflect entrepreneurial self-selection (2006). By the very act of their leaving their home countries for an uncertain future in the United States, they demonstrate entrepreneurial personality traits—a preference for the new and different, a willingness to assume risk, an optimistic passion and confidence, etc. Gartner argues that liberal immigration policies generate benefits that more than outweigh any costs associated with them because immigrants are disproportionately entrepreneurial. Shane (2008, p. 60), however, argues on the basis of U.S. Census data that immigrants are no more likely than natives to start a business in the United States. This is an area that deserves additional research.

Harken back to our example of a hypothetical search for National Basketball Association (NBA) players. If we restrict our search to prospects under 6′ tall, then we're nearly always going to be disappointed. Virtually all NBA players are taller. This makes those who aren't, such as Calvin Murphy or Allen Iverson, all the more memorable. The same logic applies to a search for successful CEOs. If we want to find successful CEOs, then we are well advised to look at the collection of individuals who exhibit the personality traits that lead to CEO success.

We all would agree that it is unproductive and silly to go fly-fishing in a typical suburban swimming pool. There simply aren't any trout in backyard pools. The remedy for those who really want to catch rainbow trout is to go where the trout actually are in cold streams that flow through states such as Colorado, Idaho, and Montana.

Analogously, those who wish to appoint a successful, entrepreneurial CEO must approach their task in the same fashion. Boards must focus their attention not only on the experience and past performance of prospects, but also on their personality traits. A candidate's experience may illuminate his or her entrepreneurial traits and leanings, but that experience, per se, may not be very revealing to a board seeking to make an appointment if that experience is couched in terms of degrees earned and years spent in a variety of positions. Even a past record of involvement with a firm that has recorded profit and sales growth may not tell us what we really need to know. The salient point is that such evidence will not disclose the heritable personality traits that behavioral genetics research and our survey data reveal are critical to entrepreneurial leadership.

The task of appointing a great leader, then, is to go where the fish are, metaphorically speaking. This will maximize (though not guarantee) the selection of a vigorous, entrepreneurial, successful leader. This is the subject we address in the next section.

HOW TO FIND AND APPOINT AN ENTREPRENEURIAL LEADER: THREE STEPS

First, let's recognize that even though our aim is to appoint an entrepreneurial leader who will achieve outstanding success, frequently only a subset of individuals will meet the minimum qualifications for the position we seek to fill. If the President of the United States is seeking a Chairman for the Joint Chiefs of Staff, then that individual not only must come from the military establishment, but presumably also must already occupy the position of general or admiral. We might go beyond this in terms of specifications, but the point is that in most searches for individuals who will occupy leadership positions, there usually are qualifications that all candidates must meet.

The essence of the problem is for the responsible appointing board to be sufficiently detailed in the specification of necessary qualifications and background that one does not end up considering obviously unqualified and irrelevant applicants, but not so detailed as to eliminate individuals who may have trod slightly different paths during their careers. It is important to remember that the individuals who have unconventional career patterns often have assembled highly interesting entrepreneurial records and frequently are deserving of further consideration. These distinctive individuals often are change agents who do think outside the proverbial box while simultaneously visioning new and unconventional approaches to problems.

Father Theodore Hesburgh was not a conventional academic, but he turned out to be a charismatic and transformational president for the University of Notre Dame. Richard Branson, the highly successful leader of Virgin Atlantic Airlines, came to fame in the 1980s as the CEO of Virgin Records, a label that acquired artists such as the Rolling Stones and Janet Jackson. Regardless, he turned Virgin Atlantic into a powerhouse and in 1999 sold slightly less than one-half of Virgin Atlantic to Singapore Airlines for English £1.225 billion. Both individuals were sufficiently different that they might not have passed muster with rigidly specified selection processes.

Nevertheless, any organization must narrow its search somewhat in order to bring a degree of order to what otherwise would become chaos. If a position actually does require a CPA (Certified Public Accountant), then there is little point in considering individuals who do not hold that qualification. No search committee should assume, however, that the paper qualifications it establishes necessarily are a valid proxy for entrepreneurial personality traits. The fact that one is a CPA does not make one a change agent or an innovator.

Second, recognize that the single most reliable predictor of a leader's performance is performance in previous positions. In evaluating the past performance of a leadership candidate, one must go well beyond the paper found in a candidate's curriculum vitae (CV) and probe much more deeply. This requires confidential, candid conversations with the individuals the candidate works with (both above and below), with the candidate's competitors, and, with industry experts who are capable of placing the candidate and his or her performance in perspective. These latter individuals often are ignored by boards but constitute a vital resource in any search.

Most candidates for leadership positions will be able to point to positive achievements—higher profit, increased market share, growing membership or enlistments, successfully completed projects, victorious battles, winning seasons, higher enrollments, etc. Nevertheless, who really was responsible for these triumphs? Were they the result of an organization on autopilot and these particular achievements perhaps even were an endowment given to this candidate by the organization's previous leader? What part did this candidate actually play in these successes?

If the overriding goal is to appoint an entrepreneurial leader, then it is crucial to determine whose role the candidate in question played in the achievements he or she cites. Was she the visionary and idea generator, or simply a vote-taking, transactional employee who kept the trains running on time? Did he embrace change, or shy away from it? Was she capable of inspiring her colleagues to superior performance? Are his colleagues and employees loyal to him and ready to climb new, even if yet unidentified, mountains for him?

The bottom line is that empirical research supports the conclusion that the most reliable predictor of a leader's performance is his or her performances in his previous positions. If a candidate wasn't entrepreneurial in her previous positions, then the odds are she is unlikely to become entrepreneurial now. If a candidate has shied away from risk in the past, then he is likely to do the same in the future. If she's been fearful of change and internationalization in the past, that's likely to hold true in the future as well. Thorough, careful, and sensitive referencing is the best way to make these determinations.

There is currently the notion in some organizations that somehow it is inappropriate to reference a candidate thoroughly. The authors encountered a university dean who regarded the checking of references and backgrounds as unethical because he thought it signaled a lack of trust. This dean became notable for appointing a senior faculty member who later turned out to have bogus degrees on his CV. Despite this, in our interviews, we were astonished to find a CEO who said he didn't pay much attention to references and background papers "because they always lie anyway."

We empathize with those who must probe intensively into a candidate's background, attempt to ascertain the facts, and ultimately make sound judgments about the candidate. It's not an easy job, but it is absolutely essential if the goal is to maximize the probability of a successful hire. Thorough referencing and background checking is especially essential if one wishes to appoint an entrepreneurial CEO. These individuals often come from unconventional backgrounds and, in any case, they don't walk around with "I think like an entrepreneur" labels on them.

Many organizations downplay the meticulous referencing of leadership candidates and instead place more emphasis upon their own interviews and interactions with their candidates. To be sure, face-to-face interviews can reveal obvious problems, personality tics and attitudes that disqualify a candidate. Still, there are two significant problems with heavy reliance on this approach. The first is that some candidates are verbally fluent (not a bad talent to have, of course) and capable of capturing their audiences with their presentations. There can be a huge difference, however, "between talking and walking" (the observation of one of our CEOs). "I'm interested in performance, not in jabber," the CEO asserted.

The second problem associated with face-to-face interviews is that research suggests most interviewers form their basic impression of the person they are interviewing in the first thirty seconds of their interview. That is, the first thirty seconds usually tell the tale and even if the interview proceeds for an hour, the end result will be highly correlated with the interviewer's first thirty-second impression, much of which is visual and has precious little to do with performance. This explains why interviews are one of the least reliable predictors of future performance.

Of course, on occasion interviews can yield useful data and they often make constituents feel good ("We got a chance to talk to all of the candidates!"). However, evidence suggests they often yield unproductive impressions and false insights. It should come as no surprise when individuals who interviewed a candidate end up disillusioned after the candidate actually has been appointed. The new leader's performance does not match his or her polished, seductive interview rhetoric.

We are not suggesting that a leader's "bedside manner" and her ability to speak charismatically before groups are irrelevancies. They are important tools for many leaders. Rather, we need to underline that there is a difference between talking about tasks and actually doing those tasks. Boards that are making appointments should emphasize doing rather than talking and should exercise great caution in giving too much weight to their face-to-face interviews with candidates. Beware the board member who opines, "I'm a good judge of character," and further suggests that a leadership candidate's character and subsequent performance really can be divined from a set-piece interview.

Third, whenever possible, accumulate additional information by having candidates complete either the short test or long test versions of the "Are You an Entrepreneur?" instruments we presented in Chapter 8. The answers provided by candidates on these exercises are not definitive and candidates do lie. Even so, our experience suggests that these instruments provide valuable information about a candidate's attitudes with respect to risk, change, and other critical entrepreneurial personality traits. An important reason they provide useful information is that candidates usually do not perceive an absolutely correct answer for many of the items. After all, they are not being asked whether they have stolen money in their current job, if they have criminal records, or if they have beaten their wife (husband) this week.

Candidates who complete either the short test or the long test instruments and whose responses suggest they are not entrepreneurial should give pause to appointing boards. If the candidate already has assembled an entrepreneurial record and the board's thorough referencing has confirmed this, then little attention should be paid to the candidate's responses here. Conversely, however, if the candidate's previous entrepreneurial record is not abundantly clear and the instrument responses point to non-entrepreneurial attitudes and behavior, then *caveat emptor*!

We now utter what one CEO informed us are "weasel words." There is no search methodology, no questionnaire, no referencing technique, and no set of interviews that will provide an infallible guarantee that a great leadership appointment will be made. What we present here is a proven means of increasing the probability of a successful appointment. The metaphor one CEO utilized with us expresses it well: We provide a means for boards to put more winning cards in the deck when they have to draw one, and only one, card from that deck. We can't eliminate all jokers from the deck, but we can increase the possibility of the appointing board drawing an ace.

A CHARGE TO OUR READERS

Management is an inexact science and airport bookstores are full of bromides telling the inexperienced how best to manage firms. Nevertheless, many aspects of management (and leadership) are susceptible to science, if only we are willing to listen to what science has to tell us.

There are some individuals who believe that management and leadership are primarily subjective activities. We agree that there is much that currently is subjective, or at least unknown, about management and leadership. Unfortunately, some who speak with authoritative voices on these subjects turn out to be substantially uninformed, or even ignorant, about what is not subjective and what science has to contribute to their discussions.

There is a visceral distaste and rejection among some individuals for the notion that aspects of behavior are genetically determined. The fear is that any admission that some behavior is genetically determined (even if environment also plays a role) might be used to justify devoting fewer resources to those who are viewed as being genetically less fortunate, or even to promoting eugenics policies.

Let us make our position clear. We are not advocates of such things. Our view, grounded in science, is that all human beings are not endowed identically. Nor, we add, do all human beings possess the same likes and dislikes. Given these differences, and based upon our personal talents and distinctive preferences, each of us tends to seek our own comparative advantage. That is, we seek to find the slot in life where we can best utilize our abilities and satisfy our own likes and dislikes. We view behavioral genetics research and our survey results as providing significant assistance to individuals (and employers, for that matter) to find the slots in life that best fit them.

We are foolish, and we risk attempting to put square pegs in round holes, if we ignore what science has to tell about the personalities of entrepreneurial managers and leaders. The reality is that some individuals are genetically programmed to be superior leaders. Their genetic endowments cause them to be more attuned to innovation and change, more likely to assume risk, and more apt to see new ways to attack old problems.

The better part of wisdom is to recognize these relationships, not to deny them. This does not require a repudiation of the influence of environment on personal and group behavior. However, it does require recognition of the scientific advances of the past few decades. We now know things of which we were not aware when B.F. Skinner was advocating his behaviorist hypotheses.

It is understandable that some writers on the subjects of management, entrepreneurship, and leadership haven't yet caught up with the behavioral genetics breakthroughs of recent decades. Nor do most individuals have the opportunity to gather data from hundreds of entrepreneurs as we have. This is not how most individuals spend their lives.

Walter Lippmann, perhaps the preeminent political columnist of the twentieth century, observed many years ago that, "Music is nothing if the audience is deaf" (Lippmann, 1929). We assert that the audience no longer need be deaf where genetic influences upon managerial and entrepreneurial behavior are concerned. You—our readers—and many other individuals now have access to this critical body of knowledge. It is up to you to utilize it. If you employ this knowledge intelligently and wisely, and if employers do the same, then we will improve the quality of leadership of all of our organizations and the benefits will ripple throughout the society.

Not a shabby outcome, that.

Appendix: The Survey Instrument

Risk-Taking in American Business

Directions

The Kauffman Foundation, the premier supporter of entrepreneurial research and education in the United States, has commissioned this study of risk-taking behavior in the American business community by James L. Fisher and James V. Koch. This questionnaire is designed to generate confidential information about CEOs and their companies. The authors completed an analogous study for American university presidents (The Entrepreneurial College President, Praeger, 2004) without any breaches of confidentiality whatsoever. The information will be aggregated and publicly disclosed in a book, but without any attribution to a particular individual or firm. The questionnaire is divided into three parts: (1) Styles/Attitudes/Values; (2) Personal Data; (3) Firm Data.

The researchers in charge of this study are

James L. Fisher
President Emeritus, Council for the
Advancement and Support of Education
1608 Weybridge Circle
Vero Beach, FL 32963
772-492-1666
tia.andus@gte.net

James V. Koch
Board of Visitors Professor of
Economics and President Emeritus
Old Dominion University
Norfolk, VA 23529
757-683-3458
jkoch@odu.edu

Questions about the study or survey should be directed to James V. Koch.

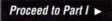

Proceed to Part I ▶

Risk-Taking in American Business

Part One: Styles/Attitudes/Values

Please react to the following statements about your own characteristics as a CEO by checking the appropriate response. Your responses should represent your own perceptions of yourself as a CEO.

SA = strongly agree	A = agree	UD = undecided	D = disagree	SD = strongly disagree

As a CEO, I:	SA	A	UD	D	SD
1. Believe that respect from those I lead is crucial	O	O	O	O	O
2. Believe that an effective leader takes risks	O	O	O	O	O
3. Encourage my firm to assess risky alternatives by quantitative methods and models	O	O	O	O	O
4. Believe that risk assessment is primarily subjective	O	O	O	O	O
5. Believe there usually is a positive relationship between the amount of risk on project and the expected return or profit on that project	O	O	O	O	O
6. Consult extensively with others before undertaking projects with considerable risk	O	O	O	O	O
7. Believe that strong boards discourage risk-taking and entrepreneurial behavior	O	O	O	O	O
8. Believe that risk-taking and entrepreneurial behavior are very difficult to teach	O	O	O	O	O

9. Rely extensively on my intuition to make decisions   O O O O O

10. Believe that I tend to be overoptimistic and that I tend to underestimate risk   O O O O O

11. Believe that I tend to overemphasize things I have seen personally   O O O O O

12. Believe that I tend to be more concerned about my losses than my gains   O O O O O

13. Believe that I tend to spend too much time on small risks and not enough time on the big, important risks   O O O O O

14. Believe that I tend to overestimate the control I have over my organization's future   O O O O O

15. Believe that I tend to place too much emphasis on my first encounter with a person or situation   O O O O O

As a CEO, I:	SA	A	UD	D	SD
16. Place a high value on consensus	O	O	O	O	O
17. Believe in organizational structure	O	O	O	O	O
18. Violate the chain of command and deal directly with some subordinates when necessary	O	O	O	O	O
19. Believe that firms often make irrational decisions when faced with risk	O	O	O	O	O
20. Am sometimes viewed as hard-nosed	O	O	O	O	O
21. Believe in close personal relationships with those who work for me	O	O	O	O	O
22. Believe in merit- and performance-based compensation	O	O	O	O	O
23. Am sometimes viewed as assertive	O	O	O	O	O
24. Frequently violate the status quo	O	O	O	O	O
25. Delegate extensive responsibility and authority to subordinates	O	O	O	O	O
26. Believe in the value of one-on-one meetings	O	O	O	O	O
27. Believe that failure of many dot.com companies provides a cautionary lesson for CEOs	O	O	O	O	O
28. Confine myself to making the big decisions	O	O	O	O	O
29. Cultivate my board consistently	O	O	O	O	O
30. Believe that the "outsourcing of jobs" from the United States is a quite valid issue	O	O	O	O	O

As a CEO, I:	SA	A	UD	D	SD
31. Accept losses gracefully	O	O	O	O	O
32. Maintain a measure of personal mystique	O	O	O	O	O
33. Frequently think outside of the box	O	O	O	O	O
34. Make a strong attempt to develop a diverse work force and executive group in my firm	O	O	O	O	O
35. Am highly involved in my community	O	O	O	O	O
36. Always appear energetic	O	O	O	O	O
37. Am often viewed as a loner	O	O	O	O	O
38. Count committee meetings as mistakes	O	O	O	O	O
39. Would rather be viewed as a strong, successful leader than as a nice guy	O	O	O	O	O
40. Work long hours	O	O	O	O	O
41. Like people who are different	O	O	O	O	O
42. Seldom speak spontaneously	O	O	O	O	O
43. Dress well	O	O	O	O	O
44. Put my company before myself	O	O	O	O	O
45. Encourage creative individuals even though they may disagree with me	O	O	O	O	O

As a CEO, I:	SA	A	UD	D	SD
46. Make decisions easily	O	O	O	O	O
47. Am confident	O	O	O	O	O
48. Believe that management skills can be taught	O	O	O	O	O
49. Have made decisions that could have resulted in my losing my job if the results had turned out badly	O	O	O	O	O
50. Am often seen as somewhat aloof	O	O	O	O	O
51. Enjoy stirring things up	O	O	O	O	O
52. Am flamboyant	O	O	O	O	O
53. Am feared	O	O	O	O	O
54. Smile a lot	O	O	O	O	O
55. Would consider moving to another firm	O	O	O	O	O

	SA	A	UD	D	SD
56. Get involved in politics	O	O	O	O	O
57. Have the strong support of my board	O	O	O	O	O
58. Have concluded many partnerships with nonbusiness entities such as universities and governments	O	O	O	O	O
59. Have concluded many partnerships with other business firms	O	O	O	O	O
60. Generate lots of innovative ideas	O	O	O	O	O

As a CEO, I:	**SA**	**A**	**UD**	**D**	**SD**
61. Am a political conservative	O	O	O	O	O
62. Avoid the media whenever possible	O	O	O	O	O
63. Am an internationalist in outlook	O	O	O	O	O
64. Support NAFTA	O	O	O	O	O
65. Attempt to get my spouse or significant other involved with my work	O	O	O	O	O
66. Am affable and warm	O	O	O	O	O
67. Believe that work force quality has declined in recent years	O	O	O	O	O
68. Frequently am seen walking the floors of my firm's offices and plants	O	O	O	O	O
69. Have much to do with the selection of the members of my board	O	O	O	O	O

	Yes	No
70. Am both CEO and board chairman	O	O

As a CEO, I:	**SA**	**A**	**UD**	**D**	**SD**
71. Am risk averse	O	O	O	O	O
72. Believe diversification is the primary way to reduce risk	O	O	O	O	O
73. Believe I am responsible for compliance with regulatory rules and financial regulations	O	O	O	O	O
74. Believe my firm can utilize software to issue warnings when unwise financial decisions are being made or certain key operating ratios are being violated	O	O	O	O	O
75. Believe my firm should insure itself against all the major risks it faces	O	O	O	O	O

76. Which of the following choices do you prefer?

$1,000 with absolute certainty ($p = 1.00$)   ○

$2,050 with a probability of one-half ($p = .5$) and   ○
$0 with a probability of
one-half ($p = .5$)

77. Which of the following choices do you prefer?

1,000 with absolute certainty ($p = 1.00$)   ○

$3,000 with a probability of one-half ($p = .5$) and –   ○
$600 with a probability of one-half ($p = .5$)

Proceed to Part II ▶

Risk-Taking in American Business

Part Two: Personal Data

My Age: [   ]

My Gender is   Male ○   Female ○

My self-identified racial or ethnic background is: [   ]

The highest level of education I have completed is: [Choose...   ■]

If your answer to the previous question was Baccalaureate degree or Master's degree, please indicate the kind:

Baccalaureate degree [Choose...   ■]   Master's degree [Choose...   ■]

The names of the institutions of higher education from which I have graduated:

[   ]   Baccalaureate degree

[   ]   Master's degree

[   ]   Professional degrees and doctoral degrees

I attended a private, independent, or parochial school prior to going to college [■]

The highest level of education my spouse or significant other has completed is: [Choose...   ■]

If your answer to the previous question was Baccalaureate degree or Master's degree, please indicate the kind:

Baccalaureate degree [Choose...   ■]   Master's degree [Choose...   ■]

The highest level of education my father completed is:

| Choose... | ▣ |

If your answer to the previous question was Baccalaureate degree or Master's degree, please indicate the kind:

Baccalaureate degree | Choose... ▣ | Master's degree | Choose... ▣ |

The highest level of education my mother completed is:

| Choose... | ▣ |

(Write answer HS, BA, etc.)

If your answer to the previous question was Baccalaureate degree or Master's degree, please indicate the kind:

Baccalaureate degree | Choose... ▣ | Master's degree | Choose... ▣ |

(Write answer BA, BS, etc.)   (Write answer MA, MBA, etc.)

I was born in the following state or country:

I have taken two or more courses in the following academic areas:

Economics ▣   Statistics ▣   Accounting ▣

Computer Science ▣   Psychology ▣

With respect to my use of technology, I:

Use the Internet frequently ▣   Use a computer frequently ▣

Carry a cell phone with me when I'm away from my office ▣   Require that the most important people reporting to me carry a cell phone or pager so I can reach them ▣

Immediately prior to assuming my current position, I:

Was working within the same company   Yes ○   No ○   Was a President or CEO of another firm   Yes ○   No ○

Was involved in a not-for-profit enterprise   Yes ○   No ○   Was in the Military   Yes ○   No ○

Other, please specify:

The total number of years I have been with this company is:

I founded or started this firm   Yes ○   No ○

Currently, I hold a leadership position in a civic club or national organization, whether or not directly related to my firm   Yes ○   No ○

I have this many [ ]   I have this many brothers [ ]   I've been married [ ]
children   and sisters   this many times

I attend some type of religious service at least twice a month: Yes ○   No ○

If I have a religious preference, it is: [   ]

Proceed to Part III ▶

The highest level of education my father completed is:
Choose... ▦

If your answer to the previous question was Baccalaureate degree or Master's degree, please indicate the kind:

Baccalaureate degree | Choose... ▦ | Master's degree | Choose... ▦ |

The highest level of education my mother completed is:
Choose... ▦

(Write answer HS, BA, etc.)

If your answer to the previous question was Baccalaureate degree or Master's degree, please indicate the kind:

Baccalaureate degree | Choose... ▦ | Master's degree | Choose... ▦ |

(Write answer BA, BS, etc.)   (Write answer MA, MBA, etc.)

I was born in the following state or country: [   ]

I have taken two or more courses in the following academic areas:

Economics ▦   Statistics ▦   Accounting ▦

Computer Science ▦   Psychology ▦

With respect to my use of technology, I:

Use the Internet frequently ▦   Use a computer frequently ▦

Carry a cell phone with me when I'm away from my office ▦   Require that the most important people reporting to me carry a cell phone or pager so I can reach them ▦

Immediately prior to assuming my current position, I:

Was working within the same company   Yes ○ No ○   Was a President or CEO of another firm   Yes ○ No ○

Was involved in a not-for-profit enterprise   Yes ○ No ○   Was in the Military   Yes ○ No ○

Other, please specify: [   ]

The total number of years I have been with this company is: [   ]

I founded or started this firm   Yes ○ No ○

Currently, I hold a leadership position in a civic club or national organization, whether or not directly related to my firm   Yes ○ No ○

I have this many [ ] children

I have this many brothers [ ] and sisters

I've been married [ ] this many times

I attend some type of religious service at least twice a month: Yes ○   No ○

If I have a religious preference, it is: [ ]

Risk-Taking in American Business

Part Three: Firm Data

The full name of my firm or company is: [_____]

My firm is publicly held:	○ Yes ○ No
My firm is a division of another firm or part of a holding company:	○ Yes ○ No
When asked what industry or market my firm is in, I say:	[_____]
My firm uses technology extensively in production:	○ Yes ○ No
My firm uses the Internet extensively to sell its products:	○ Yes ○ No
My firm uses the Internet extensively to conduct its internal operations:	○ Yes ○ No
Intellectual property and the control of such are important to my firm:	○ Yes ○ No
My firm is extensively involved in international trade:	○ Yes ○ No
My firm has offices or plants outside of the United States:	○ Yes ○ No
I own stock in the firm for which I work:	○ Yes ○ No
I am the controlling stockholder in the firm for which I work:	○ Yes ○ No
Some of my compensation comes in the form of stock in my firm:	○ Yes ○ No

The annual revenue earned by my firm is: USD [_____]

The growth rate of my firm's revenue this past year was [_____] %

My estimate of the profit rate my firm earns on the firm's equity is [_____] %

My estimate of the percentage of my firm's revenues spent on research and development is [   ] %

My estimate of the percentage of my firm's revenue earned from international trade [   ] %

My firm's two major competitors are (names) [   ]

[   ]

Many of my firm's major competitors are located outside of the United States: ○ Yes   ○ No

Here's how I rank the relative importance of the risks that my organization faces in the following areas (1st, 2nd, 3rd, 4th, 5th, 6th):

Changes in my customers and what they want   [Please choose (Rank)... ▦]

Fluctuations in interest rates, or the bond and equity markets   [Please choose (Rank)... ▦]

Increases in the prices of the things I must purchase or protect   [Please choose (Rank)... ▦]

Changes in my competition   [Please choose (Rank)... ▦]

Natural disasters, terrorism, and other unpredictables   [Please choose (Rank)... ▦]

Deteriorating conditions in society (schools, crime, etc.)   [Please choose (Rank)... ▦]

My firm's success is highly dependent upon government funding: ○ Yes   ○ No

My firm's success is highly dependent upon government regulation: ○ Yes   ○ No

My firm works extensively with colleges and universities: ○ Yes   ○ No

My firm has to train and retrain most new employees that it hires: ○ Yes   ○ No

[**Conclude Survery ▶**]

Thank you for your time and effort

Your responses will provide the foundation for our empirical analysis of the attitudes and values of CEOs with respect to risk-taking. Without your participation, our work would be a failure and hence we are very grateful to you for your cooperation.

The results of this survey, plus extensive analysis, will be published in book form in mid-2005. Meanwhile, you may be interested in the results of a similar study that focused on the risk-taking behavior of more than 700 college presidents: James L. Fisher and James V. Koch, *The Entrepreneurial College President* (Praeger, 2004).

Please direct questions to James V. Koch at jkoch@odu.edu.

Your contribution is greatly appreciated.

Notes

CHAPTER 1

1. Genetic factors do not solely determine entrepreneurial behavior. Entrepreneurial environment can make a difference. Think about an individual whose parents isolate her in a dark room, or banish her to the proverbial desert island for the first twenty years of her existence. Whatever her genetic inheritance, she is much less likely to become an entrepreneur than most other individuals. Nevertheless, absent such abnormal circumstances, previous environmental factors are surprisingly less important to entrepreneurship than conventional wisdom suggests.

2. At the executive level, the sources of failure of CEOs have been documented by Sidney Finkelstein (2003) in his *Why Smart Executives Fail.*

3. Thomas Watson, Jr., of IBM grew up in a wealthy family dominated by his father, who had founded IBM. That had very little to do with his fateful decision to invest in the development of computers based mostly on diagrams and descriptions supplied by his engineers and scientists. That decision was labeled by *Fortune* as the riskiest business decision of the era (Evans, 2004).

4. The almost accidental discoveries of vulcanized rubber by Goodyear, the x-ray by Roentgen, and penicillin by Fleming, provide auspicious historical examples of entrepreneurial and scientific luck. In such cases, an innovator encounters something he or she was not looking for and did not expect, but is astute enough to recognize its potential for development (Goldenberg, Lehmann and Mazursky, 2001).

5. Interestingly, Horatio Alger himself never did strike it rich. He only wrote about fictitious individuals who did.

CHAPTER 2

1. Interestingly, multiple studies suggest that wealth, per se, has little to do with entrepreneurship. This is true both for one's own wealth and the wealth of one's parents.

2. An earlier researcher, Nobel Prize winner Ivan Pavlov, observed that seemingly identical dogs reacted differently to identical stimuli. He concluded that factors other than environment were at work.

3. However, these "in-life" genetic changes do not appear to be heritable. Hence, the "on" and "off" changes in genes are restricted to an individual and are not believed to be transmitted to subsequent generations.

4. More than a few well-known entrepreneurs have had significant brushes with the law, not the least because they have had a tendency to push the edges of any arrangement. Consider Thomas Watson, Sr., of IBM, who was put on trial and convicted of criminal conspiracy in 1913, or Ruth Handler of Mattel who was convicted of financial irregularities in 1978.

5. "Falsify" here means that we have presented a variety of circumstances and evidence that are inconsistent with environmentalist and behaviorist assertions. It does not imply that we have demonstrated such approaches have zero validity, regardless of circumstances

CHAPTER 3

1. http://money.cnn.com/magazines/fortune/fortune500/2007/full_list/index. html

2. http://en.wikipedia.org/wiki/McDonald's

3. http://www.usatoday.com/money/smallbusiness/columnist/abrams/2004-05-06-success_x.htm

4. http://www.nytimes.com/2006/05/24/business/24board.html

5. We've performed multivariate analyses of these data and can report that the differences between the growth and profit rates of the two types of firms remain large even when a host of other control variables are introduced.

6. This is a slight variation of a conventional Likert Scale.

7. The statistical significance data were generated by difference of means tests. We discuss the precise nature of these tests, and our assumption concerning the equality of variances, in Fisher and Koch (2004), p. 53.

8. A "put" is an option that gives the owner the right to sell an asset at some time in the future at an agreed upon price. It is an excellent strategy if one believes the price of an asset one owns is likely to fall in the future and therefore wants to guarantee the right to sell it at a set price.

9. Kihlstrom and Laffont (1979) developed a theoretical model that predicted that risk-averse individuals are less likely to become entrepreneurs and our results support this notion.

CHAPTER 4

1. http://en.wikipedia.org/wiki/Mark_Cuban

2. http://www.adviceonmanagement.com

3. http://www.adviceonmanagement.com

CHAPTER 5

1. http://www.religioustolerance.org. Poll-takers caution, however, that there is a tendency for respondents to exaggerate their religious activity. By way of illustration, 17 percent of American adults say they tithe (give 10 percent or more of their income to a church), but only an estimated 3 percent actually do.

Bibliography

Acs, Zoltan J. and Laszlo Szerb. 2007. "Entrepreneurship, Economic Growth and Public Policy," *Small Business Economics*, 28 (2), 109–122.

Alexander, R.A., G.V. Barrett, G.M. Alliger, and K.P. Carson. 1986. "Towards a General Model of Non-random Sampling and the Impact on Population Correlation: Generalization of Berkson's Fallacy and Restriction of Range." *British Journal of Mathematical and Statistical Psychology*, 39, 90–115.

Alvarez, Sharon, Rajshree Agarwal, and Olav Sorensen (eds.). 2005. *Handbook of Entrepreneurial Research: Interdisciplinary Perspectives.* Basel, Switzerland: Birkhäuser.

Audretsch, David B., Werner Boente, and Jagannadha Pawan Tamvada. 2007. "Religion and Entrepreneurship." *Jena Economic Research Papers*, No. 2007-075.

Azar. Beth. 1997a. "Nature, Nurture: Not Mutually Exclusive." *APA Monitor*, 28 (May), 1, 28.

———. 1997b. "Human Traits Defined by Mix of Environment, Genes." *APA Monitor*, 28 (May), 1, 28.

Barnard, Chester I. 1938. *Functions of the Executive.* Cambridge, MA: Harvard.

Baumol, William J. 1990. "Entrepreneurship: Productive, Unproductive and Destructive." *Journal of Political Economy*, 98 (October), 893–921.

Benjamin, J., L. Li, C. Patterson, B.D. Greenberg, D.L. Murphy, and D.H. Hamer. 1996. "Population and Familial Association between the D4 Dopamine Receptor Gene and Measures of Novelty Seeking." *Nature Genetics*, 12 (January), 81–84.

Bernstein, Peter L. 2007. "Crazy Little Thing Called Risk." *New York Times*, 157 (18 November), Bu6.

Bianchi, A. 1993. "Who's Most Likely To Go It Alone? *Inc.*, 15 (5), 58.

Blanchflower, David G., and Andrew J. Oswald. 1998. "What Makes an Entrepreneur?" *Journal of Labor Economics*, 16 (January), 26–60.

Bouchard, Thomas J., Jr. 1994. "Genes, Environment and Personality." *Science*, 264 (19 June), 1700–1701.

———. 1998. "Genetic and Environmental Influences on Intelligence and Special Mental Abilities." *Human Biology*, 70 (April), 257–279.

Bouchard, Thomas J., Jr., Nancy L. Segal, Auke Tellegen, Matt McGue, Margaret Keyes, and Robert Krueger. 2003. "Genetic Influence on Social Attitudes: Another Challenge to Psychology from Behavior Genetics." In Lisabeth F. DiLalla (ed.), *Behavior Genetics Principles: Perspectives in Development, Personality, and Psychopathology*. Washington, DC: American Psychological Association.

Brockhaus, R.H., Sr. 1980. "The Risk Taking Propensity of Entrepreneurs." *Academy of Management Journal*, 23(3), 509–520.

Bureau of Economic Analysis, Department of Commerce. 2008. www.bea.doc.gov/bea.

Byrne, John A. 1999. *Chainsaw: The Notorious Career of Al Dunlap in the Era of Profit-At-Any Price*. New York: Harper Business.

Calgione, Sam. 2005. *Brewing Up A Business: From the Founder of the Dogfish Head Craft Brewery*. Hoboken, NJ: Wiley.

Canli, Turhan (ed.). 2006. *Biology of Personality and Individual Differences*. New York: Guilford Press.

Cantner, Uwe, Maximilian Goethner, and Andreas Meder. 2007. "Prior Knowledge and Entrepreneurial Innovative Success." Jena Economic Research Papers, No. 2007-052, www.uni-jena.de.

Cardozo, Richard, and Patricia S. Borchert. 2003. "The Disappearance of Businesses." www.babson.edu/entrep/fer/BABSON2003\

Carey, Gregory. 2003. *Human Genetics for the Social Sciences*. Thousand Oaks, CA: Sage.

Casson, Mark. 1993. "Entrepreneurship." In David R. Henderson (ed.), *The Fortune Encyclopedia of Economics*. New York: Warner Books.

Chen, C.C., P.G. Greene, and A. Crick. 1998. "Does Entrepreneurial Self-Efficacy Distinguish Entrepreneurs from Managers?" *Journal of Business Venturing*, 13 (4), 295–316.

Cloninger, C.R., D.M. Svrakic, and T.R. Przybeck 1993. "A Psychobiological Model of Temperament and Character." *Archives of General Psychiatry*, 50, 975–990.

Collins, J., and D. Moore. 1970. *The Organization Makers*. New York: Appleton Century Crofts.

Cooper, Arnold C., Carolyn A. Woo, and William C. Dunkelberg. 1988. "Entrepreneurs Perceived Chances for Success." *Journal of Business Venturing*, 3 (2), 97–108.

Copas, J.B., and H.G. Li. 1997. "Inference for Non-Random Samples" (with discussion), *Journal of the Royal Statistical Society*, Ser. B, 59, 55–95.

Crystal, Graef S. 1991. *In Search of Excess: The Overcompensation of American Executives.* New York: W. W. Norton.

Day-Lewis, Cecil. 1933. *The Magnetic Mountain.* London: Hogarth Press.

DeBondt, Werner F. and Richard H. Thaler. 1995. "Financial Decision-Making in Markets and Firms: A Behavioral Perspective." (R. Jarrow, V. Maksimovic, and W. Ziemba, eds.). In *Finance,* Vol. 9, 385–410. Amsterdam: Elsevier/North Holland.

Dell, Michael, and Catherine Fredman. 1999. *Direct from Dell: Strategies That Revolutionized Industry.* New York: Harper Business.

Ebstein, R.P., O. Novick, R. Umansky, B. Priel, Y. Osher, D. Blaine, E.R. Bennett, L. Nemanov, M. Katz, and R.H. Belmaker. 1996. "Dopamine D4 Receptor (D4DR) Exon III Polymorphism Associated with the Human Personality Trait of Novelty Seeking." *Nature Genetics,* 12 (January), 78–80.

Economist. 2007. "The Fading Lustre of Clusters." (October 11). www.economist.com.

Ellsberg, Daniel. 1961. "Risk, Ambiguity, and the Savage Axioms." *Quarterly Journal of Economics,* 75 (November), 643–669.

Emerson, Ralph Waldo. 1841. "Self-Reliance." In *Essays: First Series.* Boston, MA: Houghton Mifflin.

Evans, David S., and Boyan Jovanovic. 1989. "Estimates of a Model of Entrepreneurial Choice under Liquidity Constraints." *Journal of Political Economy,* 97 (August), 808–827.

Evans, David S., and Linda S. Leighton. 1989. "Some Empirical Aspects of Entrepreneurship." *American Economic Review,* 79 (June), 519–535.

Evans, Harold. 2004. *They Made America: From the Steam Engine to the Search Engine: Two Centuries of Innovators.* New York: Back Bay Books.

Fairlie, Robert W. 2007. *Kauffman Index of Entrepreneurial Activity, 1996–2006.* Kansas City, MO: Ewing Marion Kauffman Foundation.

Finkelstein, Sidney. 2003. *Why Smart Executives Fail: And What You Can Learn From Their Mistakes.* New York: Penguin.

Fisher, James L. and James V. Koch. 1996. *Presidential Leadership: Making a Difference.* Phoenix, AZ: Oryx.

———. 2004. *The Entrepreneurial College President.* Westport, CT: ACE/Praeger.

Freeman, J.H. 1986. "Entrepreneurs as Organizational Products: Semiconductor Firms and Venture Capital Firms." In *Advances in the Study of Entrepreneurship, Innovation, and Economic Growth,* 33–58. Greenwich, CT, JAI Press.

Friedman, Howard S., and Miriam W. Schustack. 2002. *Personality: Classic Theories and Modern Research,* Second Edition. Boston, MA: Allyn & Bacon.

Galton, Francis. 1874. *English Men of Science: Their Nature and Nurture.* London: MacMillan.

Gartner, John D. 2005. *The Hypomanic Edge.* New York: Simon and Schuster.

——— 2006. "A Nation Built on Immigrant Genes." *Washington Post* (April 11), A21.

Gasparino, Charles. 2005. *Blood on the Street.* New York: Free Press.

Gatewood, E.J., K.G. Shaver, and W.B. Gartner. 1995. "A Longitudinal Study of Cognitive Factors Influencing Start-Up Behaviors and Success at Venture Creation." *Journal of Business Venturing,* 10, 371–391.

Gerstner, Louis V. 2002. *Who Says Elephants Can't Dance? Inside IBM's Turnaround.* New York: Harper Collins.

Goldenberg, Jacob, Donald Lehmann, and David Mazursky. 2001. "The Idea Itself and the Circumstances of Its Emergence as Predictors of New Product Success." *Management Science,* 47 (January), 69–84.

Gompers, Paul, Anna Kovner, Josh Lerner, and David Scharfstein. 2006. "Skill vs. Luck in Entrepreneurship and Venture Capital: Evidence from Serial Entrepreneurs." Unpublished Working Paper. Cambridge, MA: Harvard University.

Hamilton, Barton H. 2000. "Does Entrepreneurship Pay? An Empirical Analysis of the Returns of Self-Employment." *Journal of Political Economy,* 108 (June), 604–631.

Hergenhahn, B.R., and Matthew H. Olson. 2002. *An Introduction to Theories of Personality,* Sixth Edition. Englewood Cliffs, NJ: Prentice Hall.

Herrington, John D., Nancy S. Koven, Gregory A. Miller, and Wendy Hiller. 2006. "Mapping the Correlates of Dimensions of Personality, Emotion and Motivation." In Turhan Canli (ed.), *Biology of Personality and Individual Differences.* New York: Guilford Press.

Hoang, Ha, and Javier Gimeno. 2007. "Becoming a Founder: How Founder Role-Identity Affects Entrepreneurial Transitions and Persistence in Founding." INSEAD Working Paper Series. Fontainebleau, France: INSEAD.

Iacocca, Lee, and William Novak. 1984. *Iacocca: An Autobiography.* Toronto: Bantam Books.

Jamison, Kay Redfield. 2004. *Exuberance: The Passion for Life.* New York: Vintage.

Kagan, Jerome. 1998. "The Nature of Nurture: Parents or Peers?" www.slate.msn.com/id/5853entry/24155.

———— 2000. *Three Seductive Ideas.* Cambridge, MA: Harvard University Press.

Kagan, Jerome, and Nancy Snidman. 2004. *The Long Shadow of Temperament.* Cambridge, MA: Harvard University Press.

Kahneman, David, and Amos Tversky. 1979. "Prospect Theory: An Analysis of Decision Under Risk." *Econometrica,* 47 (2), 263–292.

Khorana, Ajay, Henri Servaes, and Lei Wedge. 2007. "Portfolio Manager Ownership and Fund Performance." *Journal of Financial Economics,* 85 (1), 179–204.

Kihlstrom, R.E., and J. Laffont. 1979. "A General Equilibrium Entrepreneurial Theory of Firm Formation Based on Risk Aversion." *Journal of Political Economy,* 87 (August), 719–748.

Kluger, A.N., Z. Siegfried, and R.P. Ebstein. 2002. "A Meta-Analysis of the Association between DRD4 Polymorphism and Novelty Seeking. *Molecular Psychiatry,* 7 (No. 7), 712–717.

Kroll, Luisa. 2007. "Pet Projects." *Forbes*, 180 (October 15), 96–98.

Krueger, Norris F., Jr. 2007. "What Lies Beneath? The Experiential Essence of Entrepreneurial Thinking." *Entrepreneurship Theory and Practice*, 31 (January), 123–138.

Kuratko, Donald. 2005. "The Emergence of Entrepreneurship Education: Development, Trends, and Challenges." *Entrepreneurship Theory and Practice*, 29 (5), 577–598.

Lee, Don Y., and Eric W.K. Tsang. 2001. "The Effects of Entrepreneurial Personality, Background and Network Activities on Venture Growth." *Journal of Management Studies*, 38 (June), 583–602.

Licht, Amir. 2007. "The Entrepreneurial Spirit and What the Law Can Do about It." *Comparative Law and Policy Journal*, 28 (4), 817–861.

Lippmann, Walter. 1929. *A Preface to Morals*. New York: MacMillan.

Littunen, Hannu. 2000. "Entrepreneurship and the Characteristics of the Entrepreneurial Personality." *International Journal of Entrepreneurial Behavior and Research*, 6 (June), 295–310.

Locke, Edwin A. 2000. *The Prime Movers: Traits of the Great Wealth Creators*. New York: American Management Association.

Loehlin, John C. 1992. *Genes and Environment in Personality Development*. Newbury Park, CA: Sage.

MacCrimmon, Kenneth R., and Donald A. Wehring. 1986. *Taking Risks: The Management of Uncertainty*. New York: Free Press.

Malamud, Bernard, and Kevin Baker. 1982. *The Natural*. New York: Farrar, Straus and Giroux. Originally published 1952.

Maurois, Andrè. 1940. *The Art of Living*. New York: Harper and Row.

McClelland, David. 1961. *The Achieving Society*. Princeton, NJ: Van Nostrand.

McCrae, Robert R. 2004. "Human Nature and Culture: A Trait Perspective." *Journal of Research in Personality*, 38 (February), 3–14.

McGue, Matt, and Thomas J. Bouchard. 1998. "Genetic and Environmental Influences on Human Behavioral Differences." *Annual Review of Neuroscience*, 21 (March), 1–24.

Mead, Margaret. 1928. *Coming of Age in Samoa: A Psychological Study of Primitive Youth for Western Civilization*. New York: Morrow.

Min, Pyong Gap. 1984. "From White-Collar Occupations to Small Business: Korean Immigrants' Occupational Adjustment." *Sociological Quarterly*, 11 (Summer), 333–352.

Miner, John B. 1997a. "Evidence for the Existence of a Set of Personality Types, Defined by Psychological Tests That Predict Entrepreneurial Success." In *Frontiers of Entrepreneurship Research*. Babson Park, MA: Babson College.

——— 1997b. *A Psychological Typology of Successful Entrepreneurs*. Westport, CT: Quorum.

Peabody, Bo. 2004. *Lucky or Smart? Secrets to an Entrepreneurial Life*. New York: Random House.

Pervin, Lawrence A., and Oliver P. John (eds.). 2001. *Handbook of Personality: Theory and Research*, Second Edition. New York: The Guilford Press.

Pervin, Lawrence A., Daniel Cervone, and Oliver P. John. 2004. *Personality: Theory and Research*. New Jersey: John Wiley & Sons.

Plomin, Robert, John C. DeFries, Gerald E. McClearn, and Peter McGuffin. 2001. *Behavioral Genetics*, Fourth Edition. New York: Worth.

Plomin, Robert, John C. DeFries, Ian W. Craig, and Peter McGuffin (eds.) 2003. *Behavioral Genetics in a Postgenomic Era*. Washington, DC: American Psychological Association.

Popper, Karl R. 1959. *The Logic of Scientific Discovery*. New York: Basic Books.

Ridley, Matt. 1999. *Genome: The Autobiography of a Species in 23 Chapters*. London: Fourth Estate Ltd.

———— 2003. *Nature Via Nurture: Genes, Experience, and What Makes Us Human*. New York: Harper Collins.

Sandage, Scott A. 2005. *Born Losers: A History of Failure in America*. Cambridge, MA: Harvard University Press.

Scarr, Sandra, and Weinberg, Richard. 1981. "The Transmission of Authoritarianism in Families: Genetic Resemblance in Socio-Political Attitudes." In S. Scarr (ed.), *Race, Social Class, and Individual Differences*. Hillsdale, NJ: Erlbaum.

Schultz, Howard, and Dori Jones Yang. 1999. *Pour Your Heart Into It*. New York: Hyperion.

Schumpeter, Joseph. 1923. *The Theory of Economic Development*. Cambridge, MA: Harvard University Press.

Shah, Sonali K., and Mary Tripsas. 2007. "The Accidental Entrepreneur: The Emergent and Collective Process of User Entrepreneurship." *Strategic Entrepreneurship Journal*, 1 (1), 123–40.

Shane, Scott A. 2008. *The Illusions of Entrepreneurship*. New Haven, CT: Yale.

Shefsky, Lloyd E. 1994. *Entrepreneurs Are Made Not Born*. New York: McGraw-Hill.

Shiller, Robert. 2001. *Irrational Exuberance*. New York: Broadway Books.

Simon, Mark, Susan M. Houghton, and Karl Acquino. 2000. "Cognitive Biases, Risk Perception and Venture Formation: How Individuals Decide to Start Companies." *Journal of Business Venturing*, 15 (March), 113–134.

Skinner, B.F. 1974. *About Behaviorism*. New York: Alfred A. Knopf.

Slatter, Stuart, David Lovett, and Laura Barlow. 2006. *Leading Corporate Turnaround: How Leaders Fix Troubled Companies*. San Francisco, CA: Jossey-Bass.

Sloan, Alfred P., Jr. 1925. In http://encarta.msn.com/quote_561556715/Ability_Take-my_assets.

Small Business Administration, Department of Commerce. 2007. www.sba.gov.

Sorensen, Jesper B. 2007. "Closure vs. Exposure: Assessing Alternative Mechanisms in the Intergenerational Inheritance of Self-Employment." *Research in the Sociology of Organizations*, 25, 83–124.

Stevenson, Howard R., Michael J. Roberts, H. Irving Grousbeck, and Amar V. Bhidé. 1999. *New Business Ventures and the Entrepreneur.* New York: Irwin McGraw-Hill.

Stewart, W.H., and P.L. Roth. 2001. "Risk Propensity Differences between Entrepreneurs and Managers: A Meta-Analytic Review." *Journal of Applied Psychology,* 86 (1), 145–153.

Stlyrics. 2007. http://www.stlyrics.com/lyrics/anniegetyourgun.

Timmons, Jeffrey A. 1994. *New Venture Creation: Entrepreneurship for the 21st Century,* Fourth Edition. Burr Ridge, IL: Irwin.

Trump, Donald. 1987. *The London Times,* No. 62,192 (29 October), p. 8.

Trunk, Penelope. 2007. "B-School Confidential: MBAs May Be Obsolete." http://finance.yahoo.com/print/expert/article/careerist/47722.

Voltaire. 1997. *Candide.* New York: Penguin. First published 1759.

Van Munching, Philip. 1997. *Beer Blast.* New York: Times Books.

Walton, Sam, and John Huey. 1992. *Made in America.* New York: Doubleday.

Walton, Sam, and Keith E. Greenberg. 1993. *Sam Walton: Made in America.* Vero Beach, FL: Rourke Enterprises.

Watson, John B. 1925. *Behaviorism.* New York: W.W. Norton.

Weinstein, Neil D. 1989. "Optimistic Biases about Personal Risks." *Science,* 246 (No. 4395), 1232–1233.

Weiss, Rick. 2005. "Twin Data Highlight Genetic Changes." *Washington Post Online* (5 July), www.washingtonpost.com.

Welch, Jack, and John A. Byrne. 2001. *Jack: Straight from the Gut.* New York: Warner Books.

Welch, Jack, and Suzy Welch. 2005. *Winning.* New York: Harper Business.

Whyte, William H. 1956. *The Organization Man.* New York: Simon and Schuster.

Index

About the Authors

JAMES L. FISHER is the most published writer on leadership and organization in higher education today. He has written scores of professional articles and has been published in *The New York Times* and *The Baltimore Sun*. The author or editor of ten books, his *The Power of the Presidency* was nominated for a Pulitzer Prize. Among other schools, he has taught at Northwestern, Johns Hopkins, and Harvard University.

JAMES V. KOCH is Board of Visitors Professor of Economics and President Emeritus at Old Dominion University. An Exxon Foundation study selected him as one of the 100 most effective college presidents in the United States. An economist, he has published nine books and ninety articles.